WHAT OTHERS ARE SAYING ABOUT SKY ALEXANDER

Great historical family drama

The Fires of Love and Hate is historical and family drama novel and it is the first in the series of novels about Hattie, an author's great-grandmother. The story of Hattie begins to take place in nineteenth century with her forced marriage and continues with how she deals with this tough situation.

The story is based on some real characters and actual events and that is what makes it even more interesting to read. Also, the book is well written, it is inspiring, easy to read and it really draws you into it.

I highly recommend it to any fan of family, romance or historical genre.

—**Yania, Amazon review**

An inspiring read with strong female characters

Sky Alexander's "The Fires of Love and Hate" tells the story of how a strong woman deals with an unwanted arranged marriage in nineteenth century America.

The novel, inspired by the author's family stories, is set in small-town Missouri, when the state's biggest wedding is about to take place.

I really enjoyed the characterization of the protagonist, strong-willed bride-to-be, Hattie Morran, whose poor father has offered her to be married to the cruel Abner Garland as payment for gambling debts.

Although Hattie is livid she is forced to marry someone she hates, she plans a way to gain the upper hand in the situation, which eventually results in her becoming extraordinarily wealthy.

"The Fires of Love and Hate" has a few underlying themes, the main ones being optimism, perseverance, and faith.

One of the strengths of the novel is the interesting dialogue, which is both engaging and realistic.

I feel the hands-down strongest feature of the novel is its cast of strong female characters. Regardless of the trials set in front of them, they remain determined and optimistic.

Overall, I found the book to be an inspiring, interesting read that is perfect for anyone interested in the historical-romance genre. I can't wait for the next book in the series!

—**Rich Blaisdell**

Great read!!

This book was great! Captivates you at the beginning and you find you can't put it down! You feel like you are right there with the characters. Loved it!

—Jo

The Fires of Love and Hate

This book is easy reading and becomes hard to put down as you get pulled into the lives of each character. You will find yourself rooting for Hattie and her family as they overcome the many trials life has in store for them. I loved the body guards! Especially Matthew! I can't wait to read the sequel!

—**Theatre Girl**

FORCED татТо Love

Book 1 in The Fires of Love & Hate Series

SKY ALEXANDER

Copyright © 2013 by Sky Alexander

All rights reserved as permitted under the U.S. Copyright Act of 1976. No part of this publication may be reproduced, distributed, or transmitted in any form or by any means, or stored in a database or retrieval system, without the prior permission of the publisher.

First eBook Edition: 2013
Second eBook Edition: 2014
ISBN: 978-0-9915836-0-7
First Paperback Edition 2013
ISBN: 978-0-9915836-1-4

The characters and events portrayed in this book are fictitious. Any similarity to a real person, living or dead, is coincidental and not intended by the author.

Forced to Love: a novel/by Sky Alexander

Cover design by © StoneHouse Ink

Published in the United States of America

"Sometimes the worst thing that happens - is also the best."
~ Naomi Judd

ACKNOWLEDGMENTS

I, Sky Alexander, would like to acknowledge first, Heavenly Father from whom all of my inspiration comes from. Secondly, my Father Shayne Bryan Alexander, who originally had the dream to write a series that, could help to encourage people through his writing and give some light to them in the darkest times of their lives. Thirdly, my great grandmother Hattie who truly lived such a colorful life, which I would have a basis to draw from and without her there, would never have been a story to write. She was truly a woman born years ahead of her time with selfless acts of kindness and grace inspired not only those around her but her children and her children's children to this very day.

Finally I would like to acknowledge my family and friends who have supported me in the endeavor to finish my father's work and to see things through in my life's dream to be a well renowned author and like my father share from my own ideas and experience with others to help them focus and pursue their dreams. Without their help, I think I never would have seen days like these.

PREFACE

Throughout history, few women have had the money and power to make a substantial difference for good in the lives of others. When great wealth and power have been within their grasp, unbridled greed, passion, and ambition have usually walked hand in hand with them. Yet, scattered throughout the ages, truly great women have been born who, because of their very nature, rise above their circumstances and spend their lives trying to lift people to a higher level of understanding by their essence of pure unselfish love. The young Hattie Morran was one such woman, and this is her story.

Chapter 1
IN THE BEGINNING

STANDING QUIETLY IN AN UPPER BEDROOM of the beautiful Garland Mansion, Hattie Morran gazed out the open window over the lush, green grounds known as the Silver Creek Estate. Her wedding dress and auburn hair fluttered lightly in the soft Missouri breeze as she sighed dishearteningly. The cold steel of her Colt 45, nestled among the flowers of her wedding bouquet, belied the picture of a beautiful bride awaiting her once in a lifetime moment.

Without breaking her gaze, she began talking to her sister, who sat silently on a sapphire blue settee in the middle of the ornately decorated room. "So help me God, Dakota," Hattie said with great conviction, "if Abner does not come across with my demands this time, this will be the shortest marriage on record!"

Knowing Hattie was not one to mess around, Dakota leaned forward with concern. "What do you plan to do, Sis?"

Turning in Dakota's direction, Hattie slowly lowered her bouquet, reached in, and cocked the revolver. "Put it this way . . . if he doesn't, the man is goin' to meet up with an untimely death . . .

or I am goin' to shoot off the only thin' in life that Jackass holds dear."

Hearing the revolver being cocked, Dakota replied in shock, "You wouldn't!"

"Oh wouldn't I? Just you hide and watch, Sister Dear. Believe me, I've taken just about all I'm goin' to take from Abner Garland. At this point, I'd just as soon kill him than look at him! Of course, I can't do that because I love his Mama so much, and even though he is a despicable person, he is her son." With her feelings for Abner's mother, Rebecca Garland, calming her, Hattie reached back into her bouquet and uncocked the revolver.

Tilting her head to one side, Dakota let out a long, labored breath. "To tell the truth, I can't blame you, Sis. With all that Abner has put you through, I understand perfectly your wantin' to kill him. I just hope everythin' goes exactly as his mother has planned." Then, rising to her feet and walking in Hattie's direction, Dakota held up a small handkerchief edged in lace. "Is this the blue one?" she asked, staring straight ahead.

Hattie looked down at the pale blue handkerchief and then at her sister. "Yes, Honey, it's the blue one, thank you."

"I really wish I could see you in your weddin' dress, Hattie," Dakota said somberly. "It's times like this when I really miss bein' able to see."

Hattie thought for a moment and fell silent. She was so used to her sister's condition that she tended to forget how hard it was for her. Dakota Jayne (often referred to as Cody) had tragically been left blind by an unknown illness at the tender age of six, but through time, sheer determination, and a staunch refusal to be limited by the hand she had been dealt in life, Dakota had learned to cope very well.

To the casual observer, Dakota appeared perfectly normal. Strangers, in fact, were stunned when informed of her blindness, as her beautiful blue eyes looked healthy and moved about freely yet deliberately, appearing to survey everything with the thoroughness of a sleuth. In addition, the family made sure that her surroundings remained constant, and in doing so, Dakota knew instinctively how many steps to chairs, tables, and the doors. Her familiarity with her environment coupled with an extremely keen sense of hearing that allowed her to place people by the sounds that they made enabled Dakota to move about with the greatest of ease. It was only when she was in new or unfamiliar places that she became unsure of herself. On the arm of a trusted friend, however, she handled herself with poise and elegance, never letting on to her handicap. Always the life of the party, Dakota was quick-witted, had an effervescent smile, and was even a delightful dancing partner. Looking at her sister with deep admiration, there was no doubt in Hattie's mind that Dakota's strong character and deep faith in the Lord allowed her to persevere where others would have surely failed.

The silence between them was broken as Laville, their elder sister, burst into the room and rushed to the window. Raising her hand and pointing enthusiastically at the guests who were arriving, she exclaimed, "Hattie! Hattie! You won't believe who just arrived! It's the Governor, his wife, and their party from the Capitol!"

Before Hattie could respond, Rebecca Garland and Hattie's mother, Minerva Morran, entered the room as well. Rebecca, a dainty woman with blonde, flowing hair, pale blue eyes, and fair complexion, was the epitome of elegance. Smiling brightly, she replied to Laville's youthful enthusiasm with her patented southern flair. "I should certainly hope so! I invited him, as well as many other dignitaries of Missouri society. This will, after all, be the state's most prominent wedding of the year."

Rebecca was right; the wedding between her son, Abner, and the beautiful, young Miss Hattie Morran was indeed known as the social event of the summer of 1896. Rebecca had spared no expense and Minerva had left no stone unturned in making this mockery of a wedding appear genuine.

Joining Laville and Hattie at the window, the two mothers looked down over the stunning gardens of Silver Creek. The gardens were by far the most awe-inspiring part of the estate, as they were the home to nearly every tree, shrub, and flower known to man. Rebecca went to great lengths to keep the vast gardens immaculately maintained, and in doing so, it was often referred to by the locals from the nearby town of Gallatin as a latter-day 'Garden of Eden'. For today, however, the usually tranquil gardens were alive with activity, as they served as a magnificent backdrop for the wedding.

Gazing down into the shaded court area, Rebecca secretly wondered if there would be enough seating, as it appeared there were more people arriving than had been invited. But then, as if she had been reading Rebecca's mind, Minerva nodded her head reassuringly and whispered, "Everythin' is perfect." It was a beautiful sunny day this July 25, and the illusion that they had worked so hard to create was at last complete.

Turning their attention from the outside, Rebecca and Minerva set their gazes upon Hattie. Moving directly in front of the young bride-to-be, the two mothers looked adoringly at Hattie, bathed in the morning sunlight. It's warm, gentle rays streamed through the open window, surrounding her in a soft, white aura, perfectly accentuating her auburn hair. A petite girl with a tiny nineteen inch waist, Hattie stood only five foot two inches tall. On this day, however, with the morning sunlight cascading down around her in such splendid grandeur, she appeared larger than life. Rebecca sighed as she took in the picture of beauty in front of her. "Hattie, my dear, you are breathtaking."

Flattered, Hattie smiled graciously, turned, and looked outside again. She, like the rest of the family, could not get enough of the elegance of Silver Creek.

During the next few minutes, the women busied themselves making final touches on the wedding dress. As they did, Hattie's mother, Minerva, a moral, strong-willed woman with dark brown hair and blue eyes, thought back to the terrible morning when her husband, Newton, an immoral, average-sized man with red-brown hair, brown eyes, and rugged masculine features, informed her of the circumstances which eventually led up to this whole sordid affair. In her mind, she could still hear him screaming at her as she sat silently at the kitchen table, turning her coffee cup around and around in her hands.

Pacing back and forth like a caged lion in the small kitchen of their modest farmhouse, Newton's voice boomed like thunder. "Damn it, Minerva, do you hear me? Hattie has no choice in the matter! She will marry Abner, and that's all there is to it!"

Aghast at her husband's behavior, Minerva implored, "Stop screamin' at me, Newton! And lower your voice, the girls are still in bed." He glared at her with eyes as cold as a Siberian winter as she pleaded desperately. "Tell me, Newton, how in the world did you ever get yourself into such a mess, and why in heaven's name did you involve Hattie? She is only fifteen and too young to marry anyone, let alone the likes of Abner Garland!"

"And just what the hell is wrong with Abner? His mother, Rebecca, is your best friend. The boy's well educated, and he comes from the wealthiest family in the state of Missouri, if not the whole damn country!"

Minerva knew trying to reason with Newton once he'd made up his mind on something was like beating her head against a brick wall. "What's that got to do with the kind of man he is, Newt? As I recall, you used these same words last year when you tried to convince me to let Laville marry John Anderson, and look what a horrible mess that turned out to be."

Disgusted, Newton muttered, "Hattie ain't nothin' like Laville, and you know it." Walking to the open back door and venting his frustration, he kicked it shut, shaking the walls of the kitchen. "You know damn well Laville never intended to cooperate with me."

"And just what makes you think Hattie will?"

"Hattie's always been obedient. She'll do exactly as she's told."

"And what do you have your money grubbin' hands after this time, Newton?"

"Never you mind!"

Disgusted that he wouldn't level with her, Minerva slammed her cup down and held the determination of an ox. Weary of her husband's deplorable behavior, she had taken all she was going to take. "Well, the fact of the matter is that she's only fifteen years old. As for Abner's mother, she may be my best friend and Heaven knows she loves Hattie like her own, but what has that got to do with your puttin' our daughter in the hands of a man like Abner? You know, just as I do, that Rebecca had to send him back East to school because she and Jess couldn't do a thin' with him. He's worthless, Newton, and you know it!"

Feeling he was losing ground, Newton tried another tactic. "Now Minerva, you're takin' this all wrong."

"Oh, no, I'm not!" Minerva replied in anger. "Hattie ain't somethin' for you to bargain with, especially if it's to get you out of some kind of trouble. I won't stand for it!"

Newton was absolutely furious as he glared at her and again raised his voice. "Listen, Woman, I'm not askin' you for your permission! I'm tellin' you! Hattie *will* marry Abner Garland! I've already given Jess my word on it."

Minerva pushed her chair away from the table and stood in defiance before her husband. "Your word! Hah! Since when has your word ever amounted to anythin'? Get this through your thick skull, Newton. The only way she'll marry Abner is over my dead body!"

In the bedroom above the kitchen, Hattie, Dakota, and Laville listened in disbelief. Laville turned to Hattie. "Did I hear what I thought I heard? Please tell me this isn't happening again!"

Angrily throwing her hairbrush on the bed, Hattie tried in vain to control her emotions. "You heard right, Sis. It looks likes Pa ain't gonna be happy till he ruins all our lives!"

Worried for the safety of their mother, Dakota tried to calm her sisters. "Look, you two, I know you're both angry, but I think we better get downstairs. Laville, find Curtis and have him go for the boys. I heard them leave for town a while ago, but they couldn't have gotten far. I got a feelin' we'd better get 'em back to the house before this all blows up in Mama's face."

As Laville opened the door to Curtis's room, she found him frightened and huddled with his three younger brothers on the floor. He, like them, was tired of being scared of their tyrannical father.

With urgency in her voice, Laville instructed, "Curtis, go after your older brothers, and make it fast. They're on their way to town, but you should be able to catch them if you hurry. Don't bother going down the stairs and through the kitchen. Instead, crawl out your bedroom window, across the roof, and onto the shed. Take my buggy; Robert said he would have it ready for me early this morning. When you find the boys, tell them I said to hightail it back here as fast as they can. Then, get right back up here and make sure that Mark, Barry, and Miles stay safe."

Curtis, sensing the seriousness in his sister's voice, was out the window and gone before she could say another word. After making her way back to Hattie and Dakota, Laville grabbed a robe then waited while Hattie and Dakota got themselves presentable, as they had all been in their sleeping garments. "I'm the oldest, so I guess I better do the talking," Laville quipped, as the girls made their way out of the bedroom and started toward the stairs.

Not about to let Laville fight her battles for her, Hattie grabbed Laville's arm and whirled her around so that they were face to face. "Oh, no you won't, Laville! This is about me. This time I'm doin' the talkin'!" Moving quickly, they started down the stairs and reached the bottom just in time to see their Pa drawing back to strike their mother. Terrified, Hattie ran to her mother's aid, jumped in front of her father's flailing fist, and screamed, "No, Pa, stop!"

Following through without a second thought, instead of striking Minerva, Newton struck Hattie square in the face. The blow came with such force that she spun across the room like an out of control top, struck the wall, and fell into a heap on the floor. Laville rushed past their father to Hattie and, bending down next to her, wiped away the stream of blood that was now trickling from her sister's mouth. Angry beyond the point of common sense, Laville screamed, "What's wrong with you, Pa? Have you completely lost your mind?"

Showing no remorse, Newton stepped toward them, his hand drawn back again. "Shut up, Laville, or you'll get some of the same."

Hattie, knowing that it might come to this, had slipped her pearl-handled revolver in her robe before coming downstairs. As she reached in and pointed the gun toward the picture of evil that was her father, shivers ran down her spine. It was as if she was looking at the devil himself.

Seeing the revolver, a smirk crossed his face. "You wouldn't dare use that on your own Pa, now would you Hattie?"

"Just try me," Hattie said daringly, as Laville helped her to her feet. Then, quite abruptly, she pulled the trigger twice, splintering the wooden floor directly in front of his feet. Jumping back to the window, Newton could see Hattie's jaw firmly set and her eyes aflame with anger. "That's the last time you are ever goin' to hit one of us!" Holding her revolver steady, she ordered, "Stay right where you are, Pa. The boys will be back any minute, and when they are, we'll get to the bottom of this mess."

Testing Hattie again, he took one step forward but stopped when he heard Minerva call out his name from behind. Turning around, he saw that she was now standing in the doorway with a rifle. "Stop where you are Newton, or so help me God, if Hattie doesn't shoot you, I will. She's right; we've taken all we're goin' to take from you."

"Who do you think you're kiddin', Minerva? Why, the law would hang you."

Looking at him as if she could see right through him, she

replied, "Don't you think for one minute, Newton, it wouldn't be worth it, to get you out of our lives. I'm plum fed up with your takin' advantage of us. As far as I'm concerned, the depths of Hell couldn't be any worse than you are."

Showing no emotion, he replied arrogantly, "You can't hold these guns on me forever."

"You're right, Pa," Dakota said matter-of-factly. "We could just go ahead and shoot you. Then we could drag your body out in the woods, bury you, and all of us swear we didn't know what happened to you."

"Stay out of this, Cody; this is none of your affair."

"Wrong, Pa! Everythin' that happens to us is my affair. Don't think we didn't learn our lesson after what you did to Laville. No one said anythin' when you married her off to John Anderson. But this time we ain't standin' by while you try to ruin Hattie's life, too. How do you think we felt when we found out that you forced Laville into marryin' John just so you could get your hands on their farmland?"

Before he could answer, the back door swung open and Newton's three older sons, Shannon, Robert, and John, stepped inside the kitchen. Shannon, being the eldest, was very protective of his mother and sisters. Demanding an answer, he asked, "What the hell's goin' on, Pa?"

Crossing his arms in front of him, Newton refused to speak. Gaining composure, Minerva explained the situation, and as she did, the boys became enraged. Taking in all that his mother had to say, Shannon could only shake his head in disbelief. "What are you after this time, Pa?"

Newton had a reluctant look on his face, but he knew now with the whole family present he'd have to fess up. "If you must know, I owe Jess Garland a lot of money."

Shannon's blood was boiling. "You can't keep expectin' the family to bail you out every time you get yourself into trouble, Pa. We love Hattie too much to see you use her to pay off your gamblin' debts."

Newton glared at his eldest son. "She has too as she's what Abner wants, and if I was to give him everythin' we owned, it still wouldn't be enough."

"My God, Newt! How could you do such a thin'? How much do you owe 'em?" Minerva questioned, heartsick.

"More than we got. But that ain't all. Jess said if Hattie doesn't marry Abner, Laville and Dakota just might meet up with some sort of accident." Newton was lying, but with the whole family in opposition of him, he was desperate.

Stepping farther into the kitchen, John couldn't help but think that there had to be a better way to solve the situation. "Why don't we just go to the Sheriff, Pa, and explain the whole thin'?"

Thinking quickly, Newton retorted, "Wouldn't do us a bit of good. It'll just be our word against theirs, and they carry a lot of weight in this county."

Discouraged but not willing to give up, Minerva slowly lowered her rifle. "I'll go to Rebecca myself."

"I wouldn't if I were you. She can't control Jess or Abner, and you know it."

"Then it's hopeless," she conceded, her voice full of despair.

Newton, seeing things turning in his favor, took advantage of the situation. "As I see it, we ain't got no choice in the matter. No choice at all."

Hattie looked at Laville, then Dakota, who were both now sitting at the old wooden table in the middle of the room and couldn't bear the thought of anything happening to them. Seeing no other solution and wanting desperately to protect her family, she said reluctantly, "If that is what it will take to get us out of this mess, then . . . then I'll marry him."

Enraged by the idea of Hattie in Abner's clutches, Shannon and Robert cried out, "No!" Robert, racing to Hattie's side, put his hands on her shoulders and pleaded, "You don't know him like we do." Looking down into her innocent, green eyes, he continued, "There are people in this county who say that he is worse than the devil himself."

Tears begin to run down the side of Hattie's cheeks. "What else can we do, Robert?"

"I don't know, but there must be somethin'." Feeling sick to his stomach, he turned to Newton. "How could you have gotten us into this, Pa? Ain't it bad enough that we suffered shame before the whole county when you married Laville off to John Anderson?"

Again, Newton showed no emotion. "For hell's sake, how long are you all gonna hold on to that? It's in the past, and it does none of you any good to keep rehashin' it. Forget about it and move on. Now," he said calmly, "I'm ridin' over to the Garland Estate to tell Jess and Abner that Hattie is agreeable to the marriage."

Angrily, the whole family again began to protest, but Hattie raised her hands and shouted to get their attention. "Wait! Everyone wait! This is my decision, and I said I'd do it. There's no sense arguin' about it. I'm not about to stand by and watch somethin' happen to Laville, Dakota, or anyone else in this family. Go on, Pa, tell 'em, but mark my words, this ain't over between you and me, not by a long shot."

Newton, satisfied that he at last had won, turned to leave.

"Just a minute, Newt," Minerva said with a sudden coldness in her voice. Turning, he looked at her as she walked toward him, rifle still in hand. Speaking in a firm clear voice, she said, "I have one more thin' to say to you, and I'm goin' to say it in front of the kids, so they'll know exactly what I've said." With everyone's undivided attention, she continued. "I'm leavin' you, Newt, and I'm goin' to get a divorce. Furthermore, I'll not spend another night under the same roof with you. You can have the farm and most everythin' on it. The kids and I will take what's ours and be gone before you get back. We'll stay at my brother's farm on the other side of Gallatin."

Hattie looked at her mother in total amazement. "Divorce?" she thought to herself. "I can't believe what I'm hearin'." Besides her brother, Robert, whose circumstances were extreme, Hattie hardly knew anyone who was divorced. She knew several families whose fathers had run off and left them, but their mothers still never got a divorce. People just didn't do things like that.

"So, Minerva, found you another man?" Newton interrogated arrogantly.

Shannon and Robert stepped toward him, their eyes aflame with anger. They weren't about to let their Pa insult their mother like that. "Stop right where you are, boys," Minerva insisted. Newton's remark had made her furious too, but she wasn't going to let them get into a battle with their Pa at this point. "What a stupid thin' to say, Newt. I'm not about to let you make me look like some harlot in the eyes of our kids. I have given birth to thirteen children, and together, the kids and I have run this farm. With very little help from you, I might add. Tell me, where would I ever get time to look for another man?"

Newton, knowing she was right, refused to answer and turned again to leave. With his back to her, he stated coldly, "I'm goin' to Silver Creek to talk to Jess and Abner. You take these damn kids like you said and be out of here by the time I get back. As far as I'm concerned, if I see any of you again, it'll be too damn soon!" With that, he went out the back door, mounted his horse, and rode off in the direction of Silver Creek. Watching him leave, something told Hattie that the Morran family would never be the same again.

Minerva looked into the faces of her children one at a time. "I'm sorry, kids," she said with in a somber voice, "I certainly haven't done you any favors by livin' with your Pa all these years. You really deserved a better father than what he's been." Shaking her head discouragingly, she slowly sat down at the table.

Still in shock over all that had just happened, no one spoke for several minutes. Finally, Dakota placed her hand on her mother's shoulder as Shannon knelt next to her on one knee. Speaking softly, Dakota said, "It's all right, Mama, we all know you've done the best you could under the most difficult circumstances. We're a family; the boys and I will help you on Uncle Paul's farm. You won't have to worry about anythin'. Come now, let's get our thin's together and leave."

Feeling great compassion for his mother, Shannon squeezed her hand lovingly. Many times as a child, he had seen his Pa backhand his mother, which had sent her sprawling helplessly across the floor. Since then, however, he and his brothers had grown older and physically stronger than their Pa, causing Newton to be too afraid to be abusive when they were in the house.

In less than an hour, the boys had brought several wagons around and had them loaded. Seeing the house with all of their belongings taken out, Minerva turned to look at her ten beautiful children. "Are you sure you have everythin' you want, kids?" They all nodded yes, except for Laville.

"Are you positive this is what you want to do, Mama?"

"Absolutely. Once we leave, I never want to come back here again. There are just too many bad memories." Then, with a heavy heart, she called her children to come and kneel around her in prayer. Quietly, they listened as their mother poured out her heart and soul to God. "Dear Heavenly Father, give us the strength to overcome the challenge now placed before us. I wish thin's hadn't come to this, but there are times in life when it is appropriate to part ways. I feel this is one of those times. We place our faith in you, God, and ask you to lead us, your children, on our new path. Please watch over us and keep us safe from evil. Amen." As she finished, they rose slowly to their feet and took a final look at the surroundings that had been their home for so long. Minerva, devastated, knew this was her only choice if she were to save her family. No matter what it took, she knew she had to get them away from their Pa, and as they got in their wagons and rode away, Minerva instructed her children to leave this life behind . . . and never look back.

***

The way to Uncle Paul's farm took them along the front of the Silver Creek Estate. The mansion, the most beautiful house in that part of Missouri, stood a long way back from the road. At such a great distance it was difficult to make out the figures standing on the front porch, but Minerva assumed it was Newton, Jess, and Abner. Turning to Hattie, Minerva could see the discouragement on her face. Her cheeks were still moist where tears had fallen, and her usually glowing smile was a distant memory. Breaking the silence, Minerva tried to lift her daughter's spirits. "Hattie, somehow we've got to find a way to talk to Rebecca as soon as possible. I don't know what she can do at this point, but in that house, you must have her as an ally. She's a wonderful woman, Hattie. She'll be like a second mother to you."

"Yes, Mama, I'm sure she will," Hattie replied softly. Brushing back a wisp of her red hair, Hattie turned her sights toward Silver Creek. Because her mother and Rebecca were good friends, Hattie had often visited the mansion, and through the years, she had grown to love it. It reminded her of a fairy-tale palace. The architects, she had been told by Rebecca, were brilliant men from all over the world. They used their extensive expertise to create a magnificent, stately structure the likes of which Missouri had never seen before. A grand mansion three stories tall and consisting of an unbelievable 50,000 square feet of living space. The mansion towered above the rolling prairie around it. Stunning red brick covered most of the outside, complimented perfectly by splendid white wooden trim around the windows and the doors. It was protected on its north and west side by the free-flowing Silver Creek, which, naturally, was the estate's namesake. Although the Garland's entire estate included many thousands of acres of farmland in the surrounding area, the mansion itself was seated in the heart of 600 acres of prime farmland adjacent to the creek. Along with the main house, there were several guest and bunk houses, a large barn and stable area, and lastly the illustrious gardens. It was this main portion of the estate that people referred to as Silver Creek.

As she gazed over the immense property in front of her, Hattie, for the first time, realized the magnitude of what she may have to face in her impending marriage. Knowing she would need all the help she could get, Hattie was indeed grateful that her mother and Rebecca shared such a special friendship. They had first met many years ago at a church function and were immediately drawn to each other. Rebecca admired Minerva's honesty, humor, and common sense, while Minerva was immediately impressed with Rebecca's grace, beauty, and refinement. Through the years, the two had worked to incorporate the good qualities of the other into their own personality, resulting in them sharing many similar traits. Together, they, along with a few other special women in the community, had even formed a Benevolence Society and worked hard to help those less fortunate.

Seeing how wonderful Rebecca was, Hattie had always had a hard time understanding how Abner, despite his proper upbringing and education, could be so uncouth. Jess, on the other hand, had always appeared to Hattie as a very handsome and distinguished gentleman. Tall and slender, he had dark black hair and was quite personable at the many social gatherings that he attended with Rebecca. Unfortunately, as Hattie plainly found out on this day, outer appearance does not always dictate inner character.

Turning her attention back to her mother, Hattie said, "The mansion is sure beautiful, Mama, but never in my wildest dreams did I think I would become a Garland, let alone Rebecca's daughter-in-law."

"I hate to say it, Honey, but I've noticed how Abner looks at you. I've always tried to look away because I could see the lust in his eyes, and it made me furious." Pausing, Minerva took Hattie's hand and patted it gently. "Under the circumstances, I think it's time we talked a little more, heart to heart, about things we've seldom touched on." Talking openly about the many issues Hattie would face, first as a bride and then as a wife, Minerva tried to prepare her young daughter for the weeks and months ahead. Finishing, her tone was very serious. "You can just bet your bottom dollar that he'll be all over you on your weddin' night."

Feeling sick to her stomach, Hattie knew what her mother was saying was true, but at the same time, she couldn't stand the thought of having Abner falling all over her as if she were some two-bit floozy. "Mama, I don't know what he expects, but he has no idea who he's dealin' with. I'm a proud girl, and I'll not stand pat while some sex-crazed animal tries to desecrate my body. I'm tellin' you right now, Mama, under no circumstances will I consummate this marriage."

Minerva was utterly shocked. "Oh, Dear, I don't think you can do such a thin'."

"Oh, yes I can, Mama, this is not a holy marriage. It's an unholy arrangement made by Pa, Jess, and Abner, and no doubt inspired by the devil himself. I'll be Mrs. Abner Garland all right, if that's what it takes to protect my sisters, but believe me when I say that it'll be a marriage in name only."

Minerva sat stunned. Hattie's remarks had come with such deep conviction and emotion that she knew she was sincere. One thing Minerva had learned about her daughter was when she had her mind made up about something, there was very little you could do to change it. It was one of the few traits she shared with her unscrupulous father, and even though it helped her immensely in many areas, it occasionally got her into trouble.

The rest of the ride home to Paul's farm was spent in silence, as their buggy bounced back and forth over the rough country road, kicking up dust as it went. Quietly, Minerva wiped away tears of fear and sorrow from her eyes, the worry about what Abner might do to Hattie if she refused him pressed firmly in her mind. Then, as if an angel was touching her, Minerva felt a warm feeling come over her body. Somehow, strangely, she knew things were going to work out.

***

Three days after the showdown with Newton, Minerva and Hattie met Rebecca coming out of the bank in Gallatin.

A quaint town of about twelve hundred people, Gallatin was typical for its day. On the edge of the frontier, it still had its share of scalawags and lawlessness, but as the Davies County Seat, it had the luxury of a courthouse, a jail, and a Sheriff. Couple that with a post office, schoolhouse, playhouse, several small hotels, churches, and a modern bank, and by all accounts, Gallatin appeared to be a little town with a big future.

Delighted to see her future in-laws, Rebecca embraced them both lovingly. "Hattie, I'm so excited that you've accepted Abner's proposal. We have so many arrangements to make." Her eyes were gleaming like a pair of freshly cut diamonds. Then, quite abruptly, the sparkle faded from her eyes and her voice changed, taking on a very serious tone, as she asked the question that had been playing on her mind the past few days. "Minerva, Dear, I thought for sure you and Miss Hattie would have been over right behind Newton the other morning. When you didn't arrive, I began to worry, and my worries escalated when I ran into Lucretia Moorefield (the town gossip) at the store yesterday. She informed me that you and your family had moved to your Brother Paul's place, but no one knew why. I'm afraid I don't understand, Minerva. What on earth happened?"

"There's goin' to be a lot you won't understand, Rebecca," Minerva replied sadly.

Looking at them and seeing the troubled looks on their faces, Rebecca realized something was very wrong. Reaching out to them, she implored, "I've finished my business in town. Why don't we ride out to Paul's place together and talk turkey. I want to get to the bottom of whatever's got you two looking like a couple of whipped pups. There have never been secrets between us, Minerva, so let's not start now. I've always felt we were like sisters, and with this marriage, we'll at last be family."

Minerva, with a reserved smile, nodded her head. She began thinking to herself, "How in the world am I ever goin' to explain all this."

Turning to Hattie, Rebecca pulled her close and gently kissed her on the forehead. "Miss Hattie, would you be a dear and ride with us? My driver can follow behind with my buggy. I want you and your mother to tell me the whole story on the way."

So, at Rebecca's request, the three ladies climbed into Minerva's buggy with Hattie taking the reins. "Yah!" she yelled, as she slapped the leather on the horses' backs, encouraging them to pick up speed. Her firm command of the buggy belied her age and gender.

The usually quick trip out to her uncle Paul's seemed to take an eternity. Hattie sat in silence, listening to her mother pour her heart out to Rebecca. Minerva left nothing to the imagination, detailing all the events that had transpired that fateful day. Rebecca could do nothing but shake her head, and Hattie, looking past her mother toward her future mother-in-law, could see a stream of warm tears cascading down her slightly wrinkled cheeks.

It infuriated Rebecca to no end to know that Jess and Abner were involved in another diabolical scheme. It seemed like she was always following after them, cleaning up their messes, and Newton was no better. She had been aware of how mean Newton had been to Minerva for quite some time. It had only been a year ago when Minerva, with her youngest son, Miles, cradled in her arms, ran out into the rain and through the fields to Rebecca's home after Newton had beaten her. They remained for several days, giving Newton time to cool down. All of Minerva's other children had been at Paul's, helping him on the farm and were completely unaware of what had happened at home until later.

The next time Rebecca saw Newton she gave him a piece of her mind, threatening to have him run out of the county if he as much as laid a hand on Minerva again. Newton had never seen a woman of Rebecca's breeding so upset, and he knew that she had the power to do exactly what she threatened. Since that incident, Newton avoided her as much as possible. One thing was for sure, Rebecca thought, "No good can come from the three of them. Something *must* be done." She just didn't know what.

Reaching Paul's farm, the women were greeted by the elder Morran brothers, and after being kissed by Rebecca, Robert took the buggies out to the barn while she joined the family on the porch. As the boys started to leave, Rebecca insisted that they remain. Looking around the farmyard, Rebecca could see that in just a few days, Minerva and her children had cleaned up the place, which was usually unkempt during Paul's absence. Paul was an outstanding marksman who traveled the country exhibiting his skills as a sharpshooter. He and Minerva were very close growing up. Being her older brother, he always told her that if she ever needed a place to stay, not to hesitate and had a key made for her in the event of a crisis. Silently, Rebecca thought about how surprised Paul would be to see the farm in such excellent condition when he returned from his latest travels.

Rebecca's thoughts were broken as Dakota, who had been talking with the younger children in the yard, left them to play and joined the family on the porch. "Did you take care of everythin' in town, Mama?"

"Yes, Cody, we did," responded Minerva. "We also met Rebecca comin' out of the bank. She had no idea of the arrangement that Newton and Jess had made, and after hearin' about what happened, she wants to help Hattie and the family as much as possible."

Rebecca sat down next to Hattie, who was sitting on a wooden porch swing Paul had constructed from the abundant local gopher wood, as the family, with the exception of Laville, who had been sent to town on an errand, closed in around them, taking seats on the remaining chairs and the wooden porch railing. "You know, Miss Hattie," Rebecca started candidly, "that I have always loved you. I've told your mother many times that if I would have had the privilege of a daughter of my own, I would have wanted her to be just like you."

With a gracious smile crossing her weary face, Hattie replied, "Yes, Ma'am, I know that. I've always loved you too."

Grateful for the lovely young woman sitting next to her, Rebecca continued. "Several nights ago at supper, Jess and Abner told me that Abner had asked you to marry him and that you had accepted. At first I couldn't believe what I was hearing. With Minerva and I being such good friends, it seemed strange that she hadn't mentioned one word about Abner courting you, Miss Hattie. That coupled with your age left me questioning the validity of the engagement. I know you're mature, Dear, but I still felt fifteen was simply too young for the responsibilities of marriage, especially to anyone as difficult to live with as Abner. However, despite my doubts, I want you to know that I had never been so excited about anything in all my life, as Jess kept reassuring me that both Newton and your mother were totally in favor of the marriage." She paused, as if reflecting on her conversation with Jess. "Still, it didn't make sense to me, since you had told me not long ago that you wanted to marry Andrew Saxon's son, Ira, next year when he returned from Kansas City."

"Oh my gosh," Hattie suddenly thought to herself, "with all that's happened, I completely forgot about Ira."

"That is what you told me, isn't it?" Rebecca asked, wanting to make sure she had all her facts straight.

"Yes, Ma'am, that's true," Hattie replied, with a heavy heart. Closing her eyes, she felt horrible. Just when she thought she couldn't feel worse about marrying Abner, the memory of Ira and her deep love for him came crashing down on her like a tidal wave.

Rebecca took a long, deep breath and continued. "I wanted to come right over to see you Hattie, but both Abner and Jess insisted that I wait a few days. I should have followed my instincts, but I was so happy. I began envisioning what a tremendous event the wedding would be and started creating the guest list, expecting you and Minerva to appear at any moment. When you didn't, I should have known something was awry."

Reaching out compassionately, Minerva patted Rebecca's hand softly. "Don't be so hard on yourself; how could you have known what was really goin' on?"

"Oh, Minerva, I've known for years that my husband Jess is a scoundrel. I've also been aware of a lot of terrible things he's done since I married him. From the very beginning, my father warned me about Jess but to no avail. I told myself that I wasn't about to let my father run my life, and he didn't. But boy have I had to pay for my arrogance over that decision ever since. Since the very day I married Jess, he has made my life miserable, and I've had to pay over and over for the things he has done. This, though, forcing Miss Hattie to marry Abner, this is the last straw!" With deep determination in her eyes, her jaw became set. "Everyone, I've come to a conclusion. It is obvious to me, Hattie, that you're in love with Ira Saxon and you don't want to marry Abner, which, sadly, I can't blame you for. Hear me out, however, before you object too much, for I've got an offer for you that I hope you will not refuse."

Hattie's heart was pounding. She *was* in love with Ira Saxon, and it was true, she didn't want to marry Abner. Ira had asked her to wait a year for him while he was away working with his uncle in Kansas City. "How in the world is Rebecca going to get me out of this mess?" she wondered desperately. Looking at Dakota, Hattie saw the expression of concern on her face. Instinctively, they reached for each other's hands and waited for Rebecca to finish.

"Miss Hattie, I want you to go ahead as planned and marry Abner, for two good reasons. First of all, I love you, and nothing would make me happier than to have you as my daughter-in-law. Secondly, when you marry Abner, you will become my legal heir, which would empower me to legally give or transfer any part of my fortune to you."

Minerva's mouth dropped. "Surely," she thought, "I didn't hear what I think I heard." She was well aware that Rebecca, the only child of Robert Maxwell and Elizabeth Lightfoot, was one of the wealthiest women in the country. Robert was from a wealthy English family and Elizabeth from a wealthy family in Richmond, Virginia. Together, they had increased their own family fortunes many times over and had, at their deaths, left it all to Rebecca, their only surviving heir.

Stunned, Hattie politely tried to decline. "Oh no, Mrs. Garland, what you have rightfully belongs to Jess and Abner."

"My fortune, my dear, is mine to do with as I please. It is not Jess's money nor is it Abner's, and it would please me immensely to give everything to you. I can only imagine the pleasure it will bring me to see my fortune in the hands of a beautiful and intelligent young woman like yourself."

"But Mrs. Garland . . . ," Hattie tried to protest.

"Now, you listen to me, Miss Hattie. There are a few things we need to get straight, right now. From now on you're going to have to call me either Mother or Rebecca, but not Mrs. Garland. And from this moment, Hattie, it's going to be you and me. .. against them. We'll play this 'man's game' with Jess and Abner, and by all that is holy, we'll win! When you marry Abner and become my daughter-in-law, there isn't a court in the land in which they could challenge what I've done and win."

"But what about their anger?" Hattie asked. "Jess and Abner will be furious."

"Furious doesn't even begin to describe how they're going to react. Even though I probably shouldn't, I am going to set them up with handsome allowances. What can they do? I'm of sound mind. So, Miss Hattie, when you marry Abner, I will give you nine-tenths of my fortune, and the remainder will be yours at my death."

Hattie had a look of helplessness on her face. "But I don't know the first thin' about handlin' money."

"Maybe not, my dear, but I can teach you. And James Kinnion, my trusted attorney and Dakota's husband-to-be, can be your right-hand man. Right now, I have dozens of trusted men helping me, and they will continue to help you." Rebecca's eyes lit up as she rose from the swing. "Oh, dear Hattie, the things you will learn and the power my wealth can give you will be glorious. All you need to do is marry Abner, just as you said you were willing to do. There will be no union between the two of you except on paper. I'll contact James immediately and have him prepare the papers, acknowledging that Jess and Abner will give up any claim to my vast holdings. Then, I'll have everything transferred to you as my wedding gift. You only need to remain married to Abner a year, and at that time, I'll help you file for a divorce."

Hattie was at a loss for words. Her head was in a spin, and her legs felt weak. Their family had done without for so long, and here was Rebecca offering her the world on a silver platter. She didn't even know how much money Rebecca was talking about, but she knew it was more than she had ever dreamed.

"I'll guarantee you, Miss Hattie, it'll be a fight with Abner and Jess, but, oh, what a glorious fight it will be! And when it's over, your family will never want for a thing the rest of their lives."

Hattie turned to her mother with pleading eyes. "Mama, haven't you got anythin' to say?"

Minerva opened her hands upward and shrugged her shoulders. "Rebecca has been my best friend for most of my married life. I've always known her to keep her word, and I know that she means what she says. I trust her with my life, and now, Hattie, I trust her with yours."

Rebecca spoke again with increased anger. "What really makes me furious is to think that Jess and Abner would threaten Dakota and Laville! That's just one more thing on my long list of things they've done for which I intend to get even." Pausing, she calmed herself as she looked straight into Hattie's beautiful, green eyes and asked, "Now, Miss Hattie, with all I've told you, will you accept my proposal and marry Abner?"

Hattie took a deep breath and looked around at each one of her family members. First at her mother, then Dakota, and finally at her loving, older brothers who had stayed respectfully quiet the whole time Rebecca was speaking. Hattie looked at Shannon with an imploring expression. With his being the eldest, she thought maybe he would have something to say, but he just smiled and shrugged his shoulders, as if to say, "This is your decision, Sis."

Disappointed that he couldn't help her, Hattie carefully examined the proposal that lay before her. She wanted so much for her family to have everything that Rebecca's fortune could provide, but she knew the responsibilities of something this magnitude was far beyond her fifteen years. After a long pause and with the knowledge that this was the biggest decision she would ever make, a slight smile started to work its way onto Hattie's face. Despite the obvious obstacles she would have to overcome, she could think of no good reason to refuse Rebecca's offer. Taking a final deep breath, she cleared her throat, looked up at Rebecca, and said as calmly as she could, "Yes, Mother Rebecca, I can't think of anythin' that could be more wonderful than to be your daughter-in-law."

"Superb!" Rebecca responded, elated. Turning once again to

Minerva, Rebecca had one more request for the family. "I want you and the kids to leave Paul's farm, Minerva, and move into the mansion with Hattie and me as soon as possible. I've been lonely for years, and I've decided this must come to an end. Heaven knows I have enough room in that big old house for a dozen families. At last we can be as close as sisters. What do you say, will you do it?"

Minerva looked into Hattie's eyes. "It's up you, Dear. Do you want us to accept Rebecca's offer and join you at Silver Creek?"

"I don't know what the future is goin' to hold for me, Mama, but I can't imagine it without my family by my side. I intend to share everythin' Rebecca offers me with each of you." Pausing for a moment, she lowered her head slightly. "My only concern is what will Ira think when he finds out that I'm marryin' Abner." Bewildered, she asked, "What am I goin' to do about him? I love him so much!"

Rebecca, hearing the desperation in her voice, offered hope. "We'll both write him and explain the situation; that this is a marriage in name only. I'll tell him myself that the sole purpose of this marriage is to give you my fortune."

With a look of relief on her face, Hattie reached out and took Rebecca's hand. "In that case, I'm sure he'll understand."

"You'll never regret this, Miss Hattie," Rebecca said with a smile. "I'll make you one of the richest women in this country, and I'll teach you everything I know. Just think of the wonderful things you will be able to do for your family with a fortune of your own."

Hattie's head was swimming, as there was just so much to take in. Thoughts of the many ways she could help her family raced through her mind, and once she and Ira were married, they would never have to worry about anything in the way of money. Eventually, she would have to go to Ira's father, Andrew, and his family and explain everything to them as well, but given the type of wonderful man he was, Hattie figured he'd understand. One thing was for sure, Hattie thought to herself, "I am goin' to bless as many people with this fortune as I possibly can."

Rebecca continued, "Now, Dear, I don't want you to worry yourself about another thing. Believe me, Miss Hattie, I can't think of anything the two of us and my money can't manage." She leaned forward. "But first, we must confront Abner and Jess together. The only way to make this transfer completely legal is to get them to disinherit themselves from my fortune. Fortunately, I happen to know exactly how to do it, and perhaps, we should have a couple of witnesses, like Judge Stepp and Sheriff Sanders, in addition to James, to oversee the whole thing."

Hattie didn't like the idea of confronting Jess or Abner and asked, "What do you intend to do, Mother Rebecca?"

"When I go into town tomorrow, I'll open a bank account in your name and immediately give you power to draw on my personal accounts. Then, I'll remove Abner and Jess's names, leaving them powerless and penniless until I decide what I'm going to do about their allowances. Later, we'll go to James's office to explain what we want done. It will take him a while to prepare the necessary papers for the transfer of my vast holdings into your name. Also, Lewis Beaumont is home, and I plan to retain him as an attorney, in addition to James. He is one of brightest young lawyers out there, and he will be able to work with James so as to expedite the process. He told me this morning he intends to stay home for a while, as his mother Pansy is ill.

As for a date for your wedding, Miss Hattie, if all goes as

planned, I think the 25th of July would be just perfect. That will give us just over two months to get everything organized and ready. Is that acceptable to you and your mother?" Seeing them both nod in the affirmative, a satisfied smile crossed Rebecca's face, and striking her fist into her open hand, she said with great conviction, "Newton, Jess, and Abner think they know what they're doing, but with the help of God, we'll show those scoundrels who really has the upper hand."

Chapter 2
CUTTING TIES

AS THE BEAUTIFUL, young Hattie Morran stood awaiting her mockery of a wedding, the sound of heavenly music drifted up from the ground below like feathers on a breezy day. The orchestra Rebecca had hired for the ceremony was among the best in the country, and Hattie found herself lost in the rhythmic melodies. The sounds soothed her soul, and she was grateful they took her mind off, if even momentarily, the fateful night that she and Rebecca had confronted, face to face, the evil that was Jess and Abner.

The plan that Rebecca had formulated was risky, but knowing her kin as she did, she knew she had to come at them with guns blazing. First, she had James Kinnion, Judge Stepp, and Sheriff Sanders arrive about an hour before the proposed arrival time of Jess and Abner who were out pricing new plots of land in nearby Grundy County. The second part of the plan was to have the three men wait behind some elegant ornamental screens in Rebecca's study until she called them out. Lastly, Rebecca would unveil the secret she had been hiding from Jess and Abner that would force them to sign the papers James had drawn up, disinheriting the two of them from her estate. With such respectable and influential men like Judge Stepp and Sheriff Sanders assisting James as backups and witnesses, Rebecca was confident that her plan would work.

***

"Okay, this is it." Rebecca said, turning from the window to face those present. "I see them coming down the main road." Calmly, she looked around the kitchen table. "Now, everyone remember what we've discussed. James, you, the Sheriff, and Judge Stepp, stay behind the screens in my study and don't come out until I call you. Hattie, you sit behind the desk and remember to back me up like we discussed." Looking very determined, she questioned, "Do all of you understand?"

Judge Stepp, the Daviess county judge and one of Gallatin's most upstanding citizens, was still unsure of what Rebecca planned to do to get Jess and Abner to agree to her terms. Looking her straight in the eyes, he said, "I sure hope you know what you're doing, Rebecca. The Sheriff and I know firsthand what kind of tempers those two have, and I, for one, don't want to see things get out of control."

Taking a deep breath, her voice was strong as she tried to calm his fears. "Just follow my directions, do what I say, and I promise everything will go smoothly. Now, go and wait in my study. I will be there directly with Jess and Abner."

Still somewhat unsure, Hattie and the three gentlemen rose to their feet and walked out of the kitchen. The path to Rebecca's study, which was on the opposite side of the mansion, took them straight through the massive interior of the house. As Hattie walked, she marveled at the immensity and beauty of the surroundings that made up her new home. Even though she had visited the mansion often when she was younger, she never ceased to be amazed by it. Every inch of the Silver Creek mansion, even the hallways, displayed the finest architecture of the time and was decorated in the most exquisite décor available. From sparkling crystal chandeliers, to paintings of the romantic era, to grand contemporary sculptures, to gorgeous hanging tapestries, this was, by far, one of the most elegant homes, inside and out, west of the Mississippi. Hattie felt a bit like Alice in Wonderland, completely in awe of her surroundings.

It had only been one week since Rebecca had decided to make Hattie the sole heir to her fortune, and she had already moved into the mansion as Rebecca had suggested, with the rest of the family to follow as soon as Jess and Abner were out of the picture. Yet, as she reached the doors to the study, she still had a hard time believing that in two short months, everything that her eyes were feasting on would be hers.

Back in the kitchen, Jess and Abner entered the house with an air of confidence surrounding them, priding themselves on buying a quarter section of land just outside of Trenton. Seeing Rebecca standing with her arms folded, Jess spoke first. "Well, Rebecca, you'll be happy to know that your boys bought some of the best farmland in Grundy County, for a steal I might add."

With her voice holding an indignant tone, Rebecca retorted, "Given your reputations, I wouldn't be surprised if you did steal it."

Jess's smile quickly faded as he walked toward her angrily. "And what is that supposed to mean?"

Narrowing her eyes, she tapped her foot disgustedly. "You heard me. Don't play like you don't know what I'm talking about. You have been involved in enough shady, underhanded deals since we've been married to last five lifetimes. And don't you think for one second that you won't have to face up to what you've done. Believe me, you *will* be judged."

Abner, loyal to his father, rushed to defend him. "Oh, what do you know, Mother? You can't prove anything."

Rebecca smiled, as she knew she had them right where she wanted them. "Really? Well, if you two would be kind enough to accompany me to my study, I think you'll be quite interested in what I have prepared to show you today."

As she turned to exit the kitchen, Jess and Abner looked at each other confused. Abner leaned toward his father and whispered, "What's she talking about, Pa?"

"I have no clue, but she better watch herself because I don't intend to be made to look like a fool." Catching up to Rebecca in the grand foyer, Jess turned his wife to face him. Glaring at her, he threatened, "You better watch yourself, Woman, because I sure would hate to see anything bad happen to you."

Staring back at him with ice cold eyes, she didn't back down. "Save your threats, Jess. I am in no mood. Now, keep walking. I want to get this over with as soon as possible."

In that moment, Jess thought about leaving but decided to go along with Rebecca's charade out of sheer curiosity. He wanted to see what she had up her sleeve. Had he truly known of the events about to transpire, though, he never would have entered that study, for the pampered life he had become accustomed to was about to come to an abrupt end.

Entering Rebecca's well-adorned study behind his father, Abner was surprised to see Hattie sitting behind his mother's hand-crafted mahogany desk. Turning to his mother, he asked anxiously, "What the hell is she doing here?"

"I've asked Hattie to come live with me until the wedding. I thought it would be best if we got to know each other better, and as my mother always used to say, 'you don't really know someone until you've lived with them.'" Then, with a simple hand gesture, Rebecca pointed for Jess and Abner to have a seat in front of her desk.

As they sat down in a couple of high-backed chairs opposite the desk, Rebecca closed the double doors then slowly made her way to Hattie, all the while contemplating the words she intended to use. She knew that the way she handled the next several minutes would be crucial and that Jess and Abner were not going to like what she was about to say. Folding her hands in front of her, she made sure she had their full attention before beginning. Then, with a calmness that could only come from God suddenly enveloping her, she began. "Jess, contrary to what you believe, I have been aware for many years that you are a scoundrel. My father, God bless his soul, knew it too. That is why, before his death, he instructed me to have private investigators watch over your activities so that, if the time came, I would have enough evidence to free myself of you. I believe I've done my father proud, as I've got enough dirt on you to put you away for life, and believe me, if you don't follow my orders to the 't', I'll do it."

Enraged at the accusations being placed on him and alarmed at the thought of being followed, Jess rose up out of his chair. "You're lying!" he yelled as he pointed at Rebecca. "I've never noticed anyone following me!"

"Really? Well, if I'm lying, how would I know that your regularly scheduled trips down to Kansas City weren't for the farm like you told me, but were, in fact, for you to meet with shady financial investors? Once there, you would then dump nearly all the money I had given you to buy farm equipment, seed, and the like into funding all sorts of illegal business transactions. You stole money from honest, hard-working men and pocketed huge profits, which you then used to fund your escapades here at home and abroad. Knowing I'd have to approve any money being withdrawn from the family account, you were desperate for money of your own. And as if that wasn't bad enough, you would stop on your way out of the city at a brothel, where you, from what I heard, were quite the ladies man."

A look of shock crossed Jess's face as he sat down weakly. "I've never told anyone about my business in K.C., not even Abner." Shaking his head in anger, he asked bluntly, "How in the hell did you find out those things?"

Putting her hands on her hips, she repeated, "I told you I've been having you followed for quite some time. Most of what the investigators brought to me I didn't look at, as through the years your acts have become increasingly more despicable, and I didn't want to accept the truth about your actions. I simply filed everything the investigators gave me away until the time that I should need it. And, Jess, that time is now." Softening her tone, she wiped a single tear from her eye. "The real tragedy is that you've dragged our son down the same horrible road." Solemnly, she turned to Abner. "I'm afraid, my son, there is enough evidence to put you away for a quite a long time as well."

Shaking her head, she paced back and forth in front of them with disappointment. "I always held onto hope that the two of you would change your evil ways so that I wouldn't have to use any of it, but your scam with Newton involving Hattie was the last straw. She is like a daughter to me and for the two of you to think you can just throw her life around to suit your needs is despicable." Then, with her jaw set, she stood as tall as her dainty five foot four inch frame would allow and prepared to level the final blow. "That is why I've decided to transfer my entire estate to Hattie upon her marriage to Abner, and furthermore, once you leave here today, you can both find new places to live. I will not continue to live under the same roof as either of you for even one more minute."

Rebecca's words hit like a ton of bricks, falling onto them one by one, each hurting more than the last until these once proud men were left feeling like scorned children. Jess and Abner looked at each other in amazement. Abner thought to himself, "How can she just cut us out of the estate?" As he thought about it more and more, his blood began to boil. He fixed his eyes on his mother and glared at her. Rising to his feet, he yelled, "You can't do that!"

Standing firm, she would not back down to her wayward son. Hattie, seeing Abner rise up, took out a revolver that Rebecca had hidden in her desk and pointed it straight at her groom-to-be. Seeing the look on his face, Rebecca let out a small laugh. "Can't? Let me tell you two something. The days of either of you telling me what I can or cannot do are over. I have already had James prepare the disinheritance papers, and he has brought them here tonight." With a whistle, she called for the three gentlemen to come out from behind the screens.

Jess, who had had been silently stewing over Rebecca's demands, jumped to his feet in shock when he saw Sheriff Sanders and Judge Stepp walk across the room with James. "What in the hell is this, some kind of setup? What are you all doing here?" His voice was shaking as he watched his world crashing down around him.

Judge Stepp spoke first as he approached Jess with his gun

drawn. His voice held an irritated tone, and he shook his head as he looked at a man he had once held respect for but now found himself loathing. "Rebecca brought us here to be witnesses, Jess. Given your reaction to what Rebecca had to say coupled with the contents in some folders Rebecca had waiting for us behind the screens, I think we've heard and seen all we need. Those private investigators really left no stone unturned, as the evidence is very clear and detailed, and Rebecca is right, it would put you away for a long, long time."

Rebecca watched with pride as her plan began to fit together like a puzzle. Calmly, she continued. "The good Judge and Sheriff Sanders are here because I didn't want there to be any question of the disinheritance papers' legality down the road. With their signatures and Hattie's marriage to Abner, you will have no leverage in a court of law in regards to my fortune, making the transition of my holdings to Hattie ironclad."

Seeing the walls of his wicked ways closing in around him, Abner pleaded with his mother. "But what about us, Mother? What will we do for money?"

"Trust me; money will be the least of your worries. Even though I probably shouldn't have, I set up allowances for you and your father that are more than adequate. You will be handsomely taken care of, and you will still get more money every year than the average man could make in two. What you should be worried about is your attitude." Then, sensing this might be her last chance to make an impression on her lost son, she looked at him pleadingly. "You must change your ways, or as sure as the sun rises, you will never be happy."

As all of what was happening finally began to sink in, Abner desperately reached for his revolver but stopped when he felt the hard barrel of a rifle being pressed into the small of his back. "I'd think twice about that, Son," gritted Sheriff Sanders. "You're skatin' on thin ice as it is. Don't make thin's worse for yourself by bein' stupid."

James, who had made his way to Hattie's side, took charge of the situation as he laid out several legal documents onto the desk. His stature was not the biggest at five foot nine inches tall, but he used every bit of it, as he stood proudly. His wavy brown hair was neatly combed, and his well-cut business suit revealed his strong physique. His voice was that of a deep baritone, and it boomed throughout Rebecca's study, commanding respect. "First of all, the two of you need to sit down and get a hold of your tempers." His piercing, brown eyes were fixed on Jess and Abner as they slowly took their respective seats while Sheriff Sanders and Judge Stepp continued to watch them closely, guns pointed at their heads. "Regardless of what you may think, this is not enjoyable enterprise for any of us. The Sheriff, Judge, and I are here at Rebecca's request for one purpose, and that is to make sure you sign these documents. The first document states that you willingly give up any and all claim to everything in Rebecca's estate. This includes money, land, stocks, bonds, and lastly the estate of Silver Creek itself, including the house and everything in it, besides your personal belongings. The second document states that you agree to and accept the transference of Rebecca's fortune to Miss Hattie as final and relinquish any rights to Rebecca's fortune once it becomes hers. Lastly, the third and final document states that you accept Rebecca's generous monetary allowances. For all intents and purposes, these papers signify finality, and from what I've seen in those files Rebecca left for us, you really don't have much of a choice. This is your only option. Take it."

Jess sat quietly, his mind engrossed in thought. It was obvious he had little choice but to sign the papers, but he refused to give Rebecca the satisfaction of knowing he was angry. Taking a deep breath, he decided the best course of action was to live to fight another day. Calmly, he spoke with a surprisingly respectful voice and said, "Give me the papers." As Hattie walked the papers and a writing quill over to him, he looked at her with hateful eyes and thought to himself, "I can't believe it has come to this, hung out to dry by my own wife and some prissy little bitch."

With the documents now in hand, he looked them over carefully. It was clear by the plainness of the writing there would be no getting around this in any court. They had been beat. Or at the very least, would have to wait to fight, because, with the barrels of two rifles staunchly pointed at him, this was not the time or place to start something. Being a man of common sense, he knew he would have to wait for a more appropriate time. With the reality of the situation having set in, he grabbed the quill and signed the documents. Abner sat in shock as he watched his father sign the legal documents. Then, as if reading his son's mind, Jess commanded, "Sign the damn papers, Abner!"

Disgusted, Abner grabbed the papers violently. He was a very intelligent man and didn't like giving in to anyone on anything, but when push came to shove, he was loyal to his father. He signed each document without even looking them over, and once done, he angrily rose to his feet. Looking straight into his mother's eyes like a man possessed, he yelled, "I'll tell you this right now, Mother, you may think you have won here tonight, but this is only the beginning. I'll not stop until I've gotten what's rightfully mine, and so help me, if I don't get it…" His voice trailed off. Turning to Hattie, his mouth drew apart at the sides opening up into a devilish smile. "Well, let's just say that Miss Hattie won't have a day of peace the rest of her life." With that, Abner threw the papers down on the desk and turned to his father who had also risen up out of his chair. Together, they gave a final hateful look at everyone present and without another word were swiftly out the door and out of the house.

    Rebecca stood behind her desk like the proud victor of a prizefight. Her plan had gone perfectly, and now she had the necessary leverage to phase out Jess and Abner completely. Raising a clenched fist, she exclaimed, "We did it! We beat them at their own crooked game, and now the transference can commence as planned." Gesturing emphatically, Rebecca called for everyone in the room to come in around her. Her voice changed to a very solemn tone as she looked at her friends. "I want to thank all of you for everything you did here tonight. James for preparing the papers, Judge Stepp and Sheriff Sanders for making sure things didn't get out of control, and most of all, I want to thank you Hattie for having the strength of character to stand with me against my spiteful husband and son. I know it is tough to sit idly by while someone threatens you, but you can count on me to take every possible step to ensure that you are protected. And I'm sure you can count on the men's help as well. Make no mistake, Hattie, it is never an easy thing to stand up to those who oppress you, but sometimes 'cutting ties' is necessary. I firmly believe, that with a little courage, some help from friends, and faith in the fact that Heavenly Father will always be there to help, you can do anything. That is the premise I've lived my life by, and it has served me well. The advice I give to you now, Hattie, is to live your life in the same manner, for there is no stronger ally than God. The trick is giving up control of your life long enough for Him to work His magic." Giving Hattie a big smile, she kissed her lightly on the cheek as the men watched in amazement. They had almost been brought to tears by Rebecca's heartfelt words, words that Hattie would never forget.

Chapter 3
FOR BETTER OR FOR WORSE

HATTIE STOOD GENTLY touching her cheek where Rebecca had kissed her only two short months before as she slowly drifted back to reality. She didn't know quite how long she had been lost in thought, but guessing it had been awhile, she took a second to gather herself. As she gazed around the room, she saw Rebecca by the window, Laville working on the hem of her wedding dress alongside Minerva, while Dakota sat quietly in a chair near the door. Hattie was glad to see her sister and mother working together and not fighting for a change. Happy that things were peaceful, Hattie addressed Laville. "Just think, Laville, it's hardly been a year since I was workin' on the hem of your weddin' dress. Now here I stand waitin' to marry Abner, who, I must say, makes my skin crawl every time I see him."

Getting to her feet and stepping in front of Hattie, Laville turned to admire herself in the large oval mirror before them. Taller than her sisters, Laville's long legs provided the perfect base for her voluptuous body. Couple that with her exquisite face, ruby red lips, and sparkling smile and she was the dream of every man she had ever come in contact with. Unfortunately, her ravishing beauty belied her devilish nature. Brushing her long, raven black hair away from her face and carefully eyeing her own dress, she cooed, "It's perfect! The blue in this dress brings out the blue in my eyes. I don't think I've ever looked more beautiful!" Then, with a puzzled look on her face, she turned to her sister and asked, "How in the world can you complain about marrying Abner? He's absolutely gorgeous to look at, he's intelligent, and," she leaned forward so only Hattie could hear, "from what the girls around town say, he's quite a stallion." Laville raised her eyebrows up and down for emphasis, but Hattie was less than impressed. Seeing she was getting nowhere, Laville started to back away but stopped halfway to add one last thing. "And on top of everything else, Hattie, once you marry him, you'll be filthy rich."

Hattie and the family had purposely kept Laville unaware of the agreement with Rebecca, as Laville had a knack of interfering with things, and they didn't want to take any chances by letting her know too much. It worked too, because she had no idea that Hattie, at the end of the day, would become one of the wealthiest women in the country. Rebecca had kept her promise as James and Lewis were transferring companies, stocks, bonds, and vast real estate holdings into Hattie's name as they spoke.

Laville was quite surprised with Hattie's radiant appearance and commented sarcastically, "I must say, Hattie, even dressed as beautifully as you are, you're still not quite as pretty as me."

Hattie, rolling her eyes, looked down at her mother, who abruptly stood up and turned toward Laville. Speaking sternly, she said, "Laville! For heaven's sake, what a terrible thin' to say! Believe me, Dear, we're all painfully aware that you're beautiful. Now, please move so Hattie can see herself in the mirror." Laville didn't budge.

"Move out of the way I said, so that Hattie can see her hem." Laville moved away sullenly but not before looking closely just one more time. Then, with a smirk, she joined Dakota near the door.

Stepping closer to the mirror, Hattie took a moment to look at herself. In doing so, she was taken aback by what she saw. Instead of seeing a half-grown girl like she had seen so many times before, she saw the form and face of a beautiful woman. Her wedding gown, which was made of the finest satin and lace and was created by the best seamstress in the state, sparkled. Her delicate features were complimented by her innocent, green eyes, dazzling smile, and youthful, peaches and cream complexion. Hattie stared at her reflection in awe, as she had never considered herself pretty. It was Laville who had always been known as the pretty one. At fifteen, however, Hattie's beauty was the envy of any woman.

Continuing to study herself in the mirror, Hattie found that the brilliant white wedding gown she wore was bright on her eyes. It was almost as blinding as the diamond and emerald necklace she wore about her neck. Reaching up, she touched it delicately. The necklace had once belonged to her great-grandmother, Miranda Moore, a woman of gypsy descent, and was said to have once belonged to royalty. The reflection of the green stones seemed to catch fire as they brought out the green in Hattie's eyes. Her mother had kept the necklace hidden from her Pa all their married life for fear that Newton would sell it. With their having been dirt poor, Minerva knew that Newton would sell anything for a price, including his own daughters.

Laville crossed the room to the window and stood by Rebecca, who was making sure things were going smoothly in the court area down below. Surrounded on its north and south sides by four-foot semicircular rock walls, the sunken court provided the perfect place for the wedding ceremony. Situated directly off of the veranda, it was large enough to hold seating for all 500 guests, yet it was designed so as to blend in with the gardens which encompassed it.

Gazing out the window and down into the great shade canopy that covered the court, Laville commented on how beautiful the hand-crafted altar looked sitting at the beginning of the extensive gardens of Silver Creek. Being the middle of summer, they were in full bloom, bursting with every color of the rainbow and providing the perfect backdrop. Laville found herself awestruck by the picturesque scene in front of her and conceded that Rebecca had truly outdone herself. Thinking back to her own wedding, Laville remembered all too well how her father had used her as a pawn to get what he wanted, just as he was doing with Hattie. Then, looking back at her younger sister, she quietly admitted to herself, "Hattie really is beautiful."

Noticing her glance, Hattie smiled and said uncannily, "You really were a beautiful bride last year, Laville."

"Please, Hattie, can't we talk about somethin' a little more pleasant," their mother interjected.

"My wedding day was pleasant, Mama."

"Yes, Laville, it was. But the shambles you made of your marriage wasn't, and I, for one, would rather forget everythin' connected with it."

Defiantly Laville retorted, "I guess you're always going to blame everything on me, aren't you, Mama?"

"There's not a soul on God's green earth, Laville, who could possibly take the blame for what happened to that family but you, and you know it. You knew what you were doin' to the Andersons, and you did it deliberately, no doubt without as much as a second thought. I suppose it was that same devious smile that I see cross your face so often that captivated them. Poor George Anderson, God rest his soul, got more than he bargained for when he agreed to have you as his daughter-in-law."

Laville smirked indignantly, "Now, Mama, Pa got what he wanted, and I got what I wanted. It's not my fault George Anderson went crazy."

Her mother didn't intend to let her get away with that remark. "Gettin' what you want! Is that all you and your Pa have ever been interested in, Laville? As far as I'm concerned, if poor old George Anderson went crazy, it's because you drove him to it." The subject of Laville's tragic marriage was turning into another heated argument between them, as it often did.

"I loved John!" Laville shouted spitefully.

"I didn't believe Newton when he told me about your marriage, nor did I believe you. You are both heartless and have absolutely no moral sense of right or wrong. You weren't in love with John, just his parents' money. You knew what those folks had, and like the very devil himself, you went after it and got it."

Tired of their constant bickering on this matter, Hattie pleaded for them to stop. "Mama! Laville! Please don't get into this today! I've got enough on my mind as it is."

Minerva had become so irritated that she accidentally yanked on Hattie's hem, nearly pulling her off the small stool she was standing on. "I'm sorry, Hattie, I just get so upset when I think of the tragedy Laville and your Pa caused."

Laville glared at her mother but calmed down at the gentle touch of Rebecca's hand on her shoulder. Rebecca's touch always had a way of calming people's nerves. Smiling at Laville, Rebecca said, "Don't frown so, Laville. You're so much prettier when you smile."

Laville eked out a tiny smile. But she certainly didn't intend to apologize, and no one was going to make her. She had never apologized to anyone and certainly didn't intend to start now.

Minerva, still a bit miffed, said, "Rebecca, I realize Hattie's marriage is in name only and what you're doin' for Hattie is your choice, but Laville stole the Andersons' fortune and that is somethin' entirely different."

"You're right. Giving my fortune to Hattie, instead of Jess and Abner, is my choice. I remember so well my father's last words to me. He said, 'Whatever you do, don't leave your fortune to Jess.' And as for leaving it to Abner, well, we all know that he's turned out to be just as bad, if not worse, than his father. To give my parents' fortune to him would, I'm afraid, be an affront to my father's memory."

Hearing Rebecca's words, Laville's mouth fell open. She was so shocked that you could have knocked her over with a feather. She had no idea that Rebecca had planned to give anything to Hattie.

Minerva sighed, wishing that Rebecca hadn't said anything about her fortune in front of Laville, but the cat was out of the bag now and what was done, was done.

Hattie glanced at Laville, who smiled as sweet a smile as had ever crossed her face, and thought, "Oh, Lord, I'm in for it now."

"Hattie is a good girl, Laville," Minerva said reassuringly, wanting Laville to know how she felt about the whole ordeal, "and I know that with a little guidance, she'll do a lot of good in this world with what Rebecca gives her."

"And I guess you think I couldn't, Mama?" Laville snapped.

"I didn't say that, Laville," Minerva replied quickly. "But you forget that I know you've never done anythin' for anyone except yourself in your whole life, and I seriously doubt that you ever will. Your marriage to John Anderson was a prime example." Getting up to walk off some of the anger she was feeling toward Laville, Minerva saw a legal document lying on the dresser, which sat against the far wall. Turning to Hattie, she questioned, "What's this paper, Dear?"

Playing it off as unimportant, she responded, "It's just somethin' I want Abner to sign. I'll tell you about it later."

Rebecca, overhearing their conversation, was puzzled. "I thought I had him sign everything we needed."

Not wanting to hurt Rebecca any more than she had already been hurt by her son's conduct, she tried to downplay the issue. "It's just one final agreement between Abner and me." But she was thinking to herself, "He's certainly not goin' to like signin' this one."

Looking at the clock, Rebecca commented, "Minerva, we don't have much time before the wedding, perhaps we should go downstairs and meet some of our guests."

Laville placed the veil carefully in Hattie's hair as Rebecca and Minerva left the room, closing the door behind them. With Rebecca gone, Laville asked, "Do you really think Abner will sign those papers concerning Lucinda Brown and her baby?"

Interrupting before Hattie could answer, Dakota leaned forward in her chair and said, "You know he is goin' to have an absolute fit!"

Turning from the mirror, Hattie replied, "I'm sure he will. Have either of you run into him this mornin'?"

"Yes, James and I did," Dakota replied. "He and Jess arrived over an hour ago from the hotel they've been staying at, and even though he is actin' like a gentleman, I could tell by the tone of his voice that he was just about to explode."

"Abner knows when he's been licked, Cody. He's not stupid, and he's not about to give me any trouble at this stage of the game." Picking up her special bouquet, Hattie patted it softly. "But if he does, I'm goin' to be ready for him."

There was a knock at the door, and as Dakota got up out of her chair to answer it, Hattie went behind an ornamental dressing screen Rebecca had set up in the corner. She had a few final touches to make on her dress before the wedding started. As Dakota opened the door, Laville was shocked to see none other than Abner Garland. His six foot two inch frame towered over Dakota's dainty figure. His appearance was foreboding with his heavy, black hair neatly combed, his jaw firmly set, and his dark blue eyes holding a look of deep resentment and anger.

Quickly stepping in front of Dakota, Laville nudged her out of the way so that it would be she who would confront Abner. Smirking defiantly, she let out a soft laugh. "Speak of the devil. We were just talking about you, Abner." Neither man nor beast frightened Laville Morran Anderson and certainly not Abner. Giving him the once over, she said sarcastically, "Don't waste your dirty looks on Cody, Abner, she's blind as a bat. Just what in the hell do you want anyway?"

"Step aside, Laville. I want to see Hattie."

"You fool! Don't you know it's bad luck to see the bride before the wedding? Haven't you had enough bad luck already?"

Shoving his way past her, he stepped just inside the doorway.

Running his hand quickly through his hair, he turned and grabbed Laville by the arm.

Yanking her arm loose from his grip, she snapped, "Back off, Abner. I'm in no mood to put up with your shenanigans."

Looking for Hattie and not seeing her, he snarled, "I said I want to see Hattie right now! Where is she?"

Stepping out from behind the dressing screen in the corner of the room carrying her bouquet, Hattie looked exquisitely beautiful. Turning toward him, she gave him an indignant smile. "Well, now that you see me, Abner, are you satisfied?"

Smiling impishly, lust filled his heart as he gazed upon her, hungrily drinking in her beauty. He knew exactly what he wanted to do to her come nightfall, and in his lust, he could hardly contain himself. Abner was well aware of his masculine effect on women, and Hattie, he thought, would be no exception. "She may have my mother's fortune now," he thought, "but not for long." Abner had every intention of getting back what he felt was rightfully his.

Speaking to her sisters, Hattie asked, "Girls, would you mind leavin' me alone with Abner for a few minutes? Wait downstairs with the rest of the family. This won't take long."

Laville protested, as she liked a good fight and didn't care where it was or whom with, but Hattie insisted that she leave and assured her that there wasn't going to be a confrontation.

As they left, Abner moved toward Hattie. Slowly walking past him to the dresser, her wedding dress rustled softly about her. "So, Abner, why exactly are you here?"

"I want to make sure you make a good impression on the Governor and his wife today. Eventually, I plan to run for his office."

"Abner, you may be good-lookin', well educated, and possess

all the social graces to be Governor of this state, but as a man, you're about as sorry and worthless as they come. The last thin' this state needs is you sittin' in the governor's office." His eyes narrowed as she spoke. "It just makes me sick to think of your marryin' me, while all along Lucinda Brown is carryin' your baby."

"What in the hell are you talking about?" he asked, eyeing her coldly.

Looking straight at him, she had no trouble finding the right words. "Don't play stupid with me, Abner, it won't work."

"How did you find out?"

"We visited with Lucinda after her sister told Laville. And believe me, I know everythin'. She told Laville, Dakota, and me all about how you stopped to help her on the road and then forced her back into the woods and raped her. Now she's pregnant with your baby and scared to death."

"This is none of your business, Hattie. Stay out of it."

"In less than an hour, I'll be your wife. 'For better or for worse', I might add. So, regardless of what you think, I do consider it my business, and one thin's for damn sure, I don't intend to let you get away with what you've done to a girl as sweet as Lucinda."

"She's nothing but a tramp," he protested.

"Oh, stop it, Abner. I've known the Browns all my life, and Lucinda is a good person. In fact, I've invited her to the weddin'. She'll be seated alongside her sister with the other guests. I'll not have that girl suffer alone and penniless, tryin' to raise your child."

Stepping to the window, Abner peered outside, searching for Lucinda, as Hattie reached for the document.

"Abner, pay attention; this is what you're goin' to do. Sign these papers before we go downstairs. They give Lucinda the right to draw money from the account Rebecca set up at the bank for you until the child is grown."

"And if I don't?"

"If you don't, I'm goin' to have Lucinda stand up before five hundred of our guests, includin' the Governor's party, and scream out, 'You may be marryin' him, Miss Hattie, but I'm carryin' his baby!' Now, tell me, my dear husband-to-be, how do you think that pearl of information would sit with the Governor? Oh, and I'm sure the press out there would love to hear all about it."

"You wouldn't dare!" he said in a threatening tone.

"Wouldn't I? Just try me. You should know me better than that by now. I've had Judge Stepp go over this document, so he is aware of what is goin' on as well. If you refuse to sign it, believe me, nothin' would give me greater pleasure than to expose you for the cad that you are."

"You bitch!"

"Call me what you will, Abner. I really don't care. Just put your signature on this paper, and do it quick, as everyone's waitin' for us downstairs."

Angrily he walked to her, snatched the document from her hand and read it. "Do you really expect me to sign this and admit that I raped her and that the child is mine?"

"Yes, I do."

"And you expect me to give her $1,000.00 a year?"

"Absolutely."

"You've gone completely crazy, Woman. I'll not give Lucinda one dollar, let alone that kind of money.

"Oh, yes you will, or so help me God, you'll pay dearly, Abner Garland!" With those words, she reached around behind her and picked up a revolver that she had placed on the dresser. Pointing it straight at his groin, she placed her finger on the trigger. A rivulet of sweat ran down Abner's forehead as they stood in silence. Nervously, he watched the hammer draw back slowly under the pressure of Hattie's grip. Raising her eyebrows up and down, she said, "You know, I'd sure hate to see this thin' go off and shoot you in your . . ." Her voice trailed off, allowing Abner time to think about things.

Abner stood motionless, not knowing what to do. He looked around desperately for some way out of his predicament, but unfortunately for him, none was to be found.

Tired of playing around, Hattie yelled, "Sign it now, Abner!"

Reluctantly, Abner picked up the writing quill, dipped it in the ink, signed the papers, and handed them back to her. He hated being backed up into a corner like this, but after all he had been through the last two months with Hattie, he knew that regardless of the consequences, she would do exactly what she was threatening.

Taking the paper from him, Hattie laid the revolver down and started to leave the room. "Thank you, Abner. Now, let's hurry along. They're waitin' for us downstairs."

Seeing her lay down her gun, he quickly moved in front of her and snatched the document from her hand. With a smile of satisfaction on his face, he said, "That wasn't too smart, Hattie."

"Think again, Sugar," Hattie said, lowering her bouquet just enough to expose the other revolver concealed within. Seeing it, Abner's jaw dropped. "Pretty clever little bouquet, don't you think? You know, I'm just a bit nervous this mornin', it bein' my weddin' day and all. I guess you could say I've got the weddin' day jitters. Why, I'm so shaky that if I were you, I'd be afraid that this little old gun might just accidentally go off. I think it would be in your best interest, Abner, to stop upsettin' me. Now hand me that document and be quick about it." Shaking his head, he handed it back to her. Then, with her special bouquet, Hattie motioned for him to exit the room ahead of her. "I suppose you've been with the Governor the whole time he's been here this mornin', no doubt doin' your best to charm him. Well, you can just bet your boots that I can charm him a hell of a lot better than you. Don't worry about my impressin' him. With your mother's fortune, it will be to my advantage to have him on my side."

Reaching the balcony above the grand foyer, Hattie saw her family waiting anxiously below. Easily the most impressive room in the house, the grand foyer mesmerized first time visitors to the mansion, who upon entering from outside through the ornate French doors, were captivated by its sheer size and magnificence. Several thousand square feet by itself, the grand foyer had an exquisite white marble floor and was bisected by an extravagant grand staircase. Starting from the second floor in two equal and opposite sections, the staircase came together half way down, directly under one of the largest and most beautiful crystal chandeliers in the world. From there, the remaining stairs flowed like smooth silk to the main floor, widening slightly at the end. Priceless artwork and tapestries adorned the walls, elegant sculptures lined the exterior, and solid oak abounded everywhere, from the decorative banisters that lined the stairs to the trim around the windows and doors. Finally, the room was decorated in a mixture of pastel colors, giving the room a very inviting feel. Rebecca was big on first impressions, and she had spared no expense in making this entrance to her home unforgettable.

Reaching the bottom of the stairs, Hattie and Abner found both of their families waiting in silence. Turning around and stepping back up two steps, Hattie placed her arm on the banister and sighed. "My, my, my, what a gloomy lookin' bunch. Why, we can't have this. We have all those people out there waitin' to see the weddin' of the year."

Rebecca quickly agreed. "You're right, Miss Hattie, let's give them the time of their lives. After all, that certainly is what I've paid for."

Standing in the back next to Dakota, James Kinnion said, "You look beautiful, Miss Hattie, but let's not keep the guests waiting."

"Sounds good, James. These people came here in good faith expectin' to see a beautiful weddin', and by God, that's exactly what we're goin' to give 'em."

Abner turned around and looked at her with contempt.

Looking down at him, she smiled and gave him a little wink. "Oh, for Heaven's sake, Abner, buck-up. Today's your weddin' day, and because of your Mama, you're marryin' just about the richest girl in the country."

Looking at her with hateful eyes, he snarled, "So you think you can fit in, you a poor dirt farmer's daughter."

"Oh, don't worry about me, Abner. I may have felt that way two months ago but not anymore. Just knowin' I'm rich makes me feel like I can hold my own with anyone."

Before Abner could reply, Hattie's brother, Robert, interjected, "Looks to me like you're marryin' yourself one hell of a woman, Abner. Best you be gettin' outside and down front before she changes her mind."

Disgusted, Abner turned and made his way through the

mansion and out the back door to the veranda, with everyone else following close behind. Minerva went first, followed by Hattie's brother, John, who accompanied Rebecca, followed by Laville and Robert, and finally Dakota and James, leaving Shannon and Hattie alone.

Looking up into Shannon's light hazel eyes, Hattie couldn't help but admire how handsome he had become. He had always been quite comely, but now, at twenty-five and in the prime of his life, Shannon's muscular physique, wavy brown hair, and rugged facial features came together to form a very impressive looking man.

"Shannon, can I ask you a question?" Hattie asked, still looking up into his eyes.

"Of course, Sis, what is it?"

"Why, after Robert's marriage and your engagement ended, did you come home again?"

"Well, as you know, Robert's wife ran off with another man," Shannon replied matter-of-factly, "and my engagement, though I tried very hard to save it, fell apart when her father died. It was a freak accident, and it devastated her. From that point on, she was a different person. Not being able to handle the hard reality of it, she decided to move back to Pennsylvania with her mother. I wanted to go with her and get married as planned, but with my job and family here in Missouri, we decided it would be better for us to part ways. Even though our situations were very different, our relationships ended about the same time. That was the year Pa was gone for such a long time and Mama needed help on the farm. We both talked it over and decided we ought to go home and help her as much as we could. Then, when Pa came home, he was so damn mean to Mama and you kids, we thought we better stick around to keep him from beatin' the livin' daylights out of you. Didn't Mama ever tell you that?"

"No, and we never asked."

Shannon squeezed her hand lovingly. "Well, now you know, but in truth, we shouldn't dawdle. I'm sure everyone is waitin' for us."

Nodding in agreement, Hattie followed Shannon's lead as he started to escort her to the back of the house.

As they walked, Shannon couldn't help but look into the parlor off of the grand foyer to the left. The most used room in the house and quite large in its own right, the parlor served as both a place of relaxation and a place of meeting, as it was where most of the important family discussions took place. In fact, there was rarely a time that someone wasn't inside the parlor doing something.

The inside of the parlor was, much like the grand foyer, adorned with only the best of modern décor, but instead of a pastel decorative scheme, various shades of blue, one of Rebecca's favorite colors, dominated the room. The far wall was home to a large, brick fireplace around which sat several chairs and settees. A black grand piano occupied the middle of the room, and lastly, standing on opposite sides of the room were an impressive grandfather clock and an even more impressive bronze statue of Rebecca's father.

The statue had been a gift to her father from a dignitary in Europe as a sign of good will between their families. Rebecca kept it on display so that, as she said, "I can keep my father's memory alive." She would continue by saying, "Too often in life, we forget those who pass before us, and in doing so, the legacy that they tried to create dies, rendering all that they worked so hard to accomplish mute. It is only in remembering our loved ones who have passed that we can honor their memory and incorporate their good qualities into our own personalities, so that we can become better people ourselves."

Shaking his head in disbelief, Shannon turned to Hattie and said, "This place is incredible, Sis. It still amazes me that in a few short hours, all this will be yours."

"It is pretty amazin', isn't it?"

"Yes, it is," Shannon replied emphatically. Then, with his voice taking on a serious tone, he added, "But as far as I'm concerned, you deserve this and everythin' else Rebecca's given to you as well."

Hattie laughed. "I appreciate you sayin' that, Shannon, but I'm afraid old Jess and Abner sure didn't think so the night Rebecca and I confronted 'em."

"I've been meanin' to ask you, Hattie. Just how did the two of you pull off gettin' 'em to sign those disinheritance papers?"

As Hattie took a moment to explain the painful details of the night in Rebecca's study, Shannon listened in amazement. When she finished, Shannon could hardly control his anger. "I ought'a horsewhip Abner for threathenin' you like that!" Then, with Hattie's soft touch calming him, he asked her matter-of-factly, "How come the Sheriff didn't run 'em in?"

"He owed Rebecca a big favor, and she called in her marker. I don't know what it was she had done for him, but it was big enough that he did as she asked in this instance."

"Why didn't Rebecca just have 'em arrested?"

"Oh, Shannon, she couldn't afford to have a scandal like that. What would people think of her, havin' her husband and son arrested? Imagine what would be written in the newspapers." Patting his arm lovingly, she said, "Trust me, Rebecca's a smart woman, and she knows how to handle delicate affairs such as these. The confessions that Jess and Abner signed could put them behind bars for a very long time, and I doubt that either of 'em will be foolish enough to test her." Pausing, an ominous feeling came over her, and for a moment, Hattie felt sick to her stomach. Shaking it off, she decided to change the subject. "You'll be happy to know that James has agreed to help me handle my fortune, Shannon."

As they neared the end of the long hallway leading out to the veranda, Shannon nodded and said, "That's great, Sis, but I knew he would. He's a good man, and he couldn't turn his back on anyone, let alone you." Taking a deep breath, he added, "I sure am lookin' forward to Dakota marryin' him at Christmas time. They really make a wonderful couple."

"I think so too. Dakota loves him so much, and havin' a lawyer for my brother-in-law is the best thin' that could happen to me."

Reaching the back door, they found Abner totally exasperated. "What the hell has been keeping you two?" he quipped.

"Watch what you say, Abner," Shannon bristled, still miffed about his threats toward Hattie. He wasn't quite as tall as Abner, but physically, Shannon could whip the socks off of just about anyone, especially Abner. Returning Abner's hateful glare, Shannon let him know he meant business.

Turning back to Hattie, Abner muttered under his breath. "I just saw Lucinda Brown. I hope you're happy, Hattie."

"Yes, Abner," she said with a sparkle in her eye, "I am." As the music began playing, Hattie instructed, "Now, get your fanny down front where you belong." Sullenly, Abner retreated to the altar and stood next to his father. Then, with shock, Hattie watched as her Pa moved out from behind Jess and made his way down the aisle to find her. "Oh

Lordy-be, Shannon, here comes Pa. Where did he come from?"

"I don't know. I haven't seen him since we left the farm."

Newton took his time, walking like a proud peacock and making himself the center of attention. Robert, who was seated next to the aisle in the audience, was disgusted with his Pa's arrogant behavior. Putting his foot out in front of Newton as he was walking, he tripped his father, causing him to fall forward and land in a woman's lap. Chuckling, he turned to Laville, who was seated next to him. "That should take the wind out of his sails."

"He'll kill you for that," Laville said, chuckling herself.

"Forget that," he replied quickly. "Pa's days of mistreatin' us are over. With all that Rebecca has done for Hattie and the family, he'll never have any control over us ever again. He can sit on that pile of dirt he calls a farm and rot for all I care."

Settling back in her seat, Laville glanced around at the beauty of Silver Creek. "I just don't understand why Hattie didn't ask me to move out here?"

Raising his eyebrows in disbelief, Robert turned and looked her in the eyes. "Why should she? You've got the biggest house in Gallatin. And as I recall, you certainly didn't ask any of us to come live with you when you bought that place."

"Oh, Robert, my house can't begin to compare to this mansion and you know it." Her voice dropped. "Besides, I'm out of money."

"Out of money!" Robert's voice boomed, not believing what he'd just heard. Then, realizing everyone around him had heard him, he lowered his voice. "My God, Laville, how could you possibly be out of money? You had a fortune."

Half-pouting, she insisted, "It wasn't all that much."

"The hell it wasn't," he said, grabbing her by the shoulders and shaking her. "I'll never make that much money in a lifetime, and you say you've gone through it already? I don't believe you."

Back on the veranda, Hattie was amazed at how many tables Rebecca had had setup for the reception afterward. Making her way across the enormous open room on the back of the mansion, Hattie had never seen so many tables and chairs. Pausing at the stairs leading down into the court, she turned to her brother John and said, "Do you see Lucinda Brown there on the aisle?"

"Yes."

"Would you be a dear and fetch her for me? I have somethin' to tell her."

"Now, Hattie, before the weddin'?"

"Yes, now! And hurry!"

Newton reached Hattie and Shannon, just as John went for Lucinda. Still perturbed from his fall, he was anxious to get things going. "What the hell is holdin' you up, Hattie?"

Surprised that he was even there in the first place, she asked, "What were you doin' down front, Pa? If you intended to walk me down the isle, you should have been here waitin' for me."

His eyes narrowed. "For God's sake, get a move on; everyone's lookin' at us."

"Of course they're lookin' at us; I am *the* bride. But don't you worry, Pa, they won't start without me." She waved pleasantly and smiled at the crowd. "Go take your place now, Shannon. Pa and I will be there directly." Newton frowned as he thought things were taking entirely too much time. As Shannon left, John returned with Lucinda. Taking her tiny hands, Hattie placed the document in them.

"What's this?" she asked, puzzled.

Hattie took her gently by the shoulder and led her off to the side so they could talk privately. "It's a document Abner has signed, acknowledgin' your baby as his and givin' you the authority to draw one thousand dollars a year on his bank account until the child is grown. Both James Kinnion and Judge Stepp have signed these papers. Believe me, Abner doesn't want a scandal. He intends to enter politics, and you can hold this over his head for a long, long time."

"I don't know how to thank you, Miss Hattie," Lucinda said as tears streamed down her rosy cheeks.

"Abner will be leavin' for the East shortly. You could thank me by comin' out here to stay with me, and together, we'll tell Rebecca."

Lucinda's head dropped, and her smile quickly faded away. "What do you think she will think of me?"

"That baby you're carryin' is her grandchild. I'm sure she will want to help you. So, what do you say? Will you come and stay with me?"

Lucinda was so overcome with Hattie's kindness that she was unable to speak.

"Well, you think about it and tell me after the ceremony." Turning to John, Hattie asked, "Will you take Lucinda back to her seat?" Then, returning to Newton, Hattie was ready. "Well, Pa, if you plan to give me away, I guess it's time to face the music." With the orchestra breaking into the wedding processional, she took his arm and they began their slow walk off of the veranda and down the aisle through the large crowd in the court toward Abner, who was waiting impatiently at the altar.

Whispering to Hattie and smiling the whole time, Newton said, "I suppose you realize this turned out to be the best thin' that ever happened to you. You're marryin' into high society, and as I understand from Jess, Rebecca has made you rich beyond your wildest dreams."

"Listen to me, Pa, even with all I've been given, this is pretty much rock bottom for me." Then, through clenched teeth, she added, "Especially havin' to marry Abner to get it."

"I knew what I was doin', Hat."

"Oh, you did not. Who do you think you're foolin'? You had no idea what Rebecca planned to do."

"You think not, Hat?"

"Don't call me Hat, Pa, you know how I hate it. And don't you think for one minute that you're the one who helped me get anythin'. I know you would have just as soon sold me into slavery if you had to, if that is what it would have taken to get that land of Jess Garland's to add to the farm. You lied, Pa. There was no gamblin' debt, and you know it. It was more land you were after all along."

Newton, surprised at her statement, asked, "Who told you I wanted land?"

"Rebecca overheard Jess and Abner talkin' about it before she kicked 'em out. Let me tell you somethin', Pa. That land belongs to me now. And believe me, you'll not get as much as a teaspoonful of dirt from it."

Hatefully, he glared at her as if he wished her dead.

Nothing else was said as they walked the rest of the way in silence. Stepping in time with the music down the red-carpeted aisle, Hattie glanced out at the clear, blue sky and took a deep breath. The morning had turned out beautifully. A soft breeze blew gently through the trees, causing the grass to move like a great sheet being fluffed over a freshly made bed. The flowers in Rebecca's gardens were in full bloom and added just the right fragrance.

Reaching the front, Hattie saw Dakota, the maid of honor, waiting patiently along with Abner, Jess, and Stanley Johnson, the prosecuting attorney for Davies County and Abner's best man. Shorter than average, Stanley was one of the only friends that Abner had. Some girls thought he was handsome with his coal black hair and muscular build, but Hattie found his personality downright frightful as he made up for his lack of height with arrogant and pompous behavior. His personality aside, though, Stanley was a great lawyer. He and Abner ran together at school back east, and once they graduated, Abner persuaded him to move to Missouri. His family lived in Ohio, but Abner promised him power and position in Missouri if he relocated. Knowing what type of money the Garlands had, he accepted, and after Jess had pulled some strings, Stanley was hired by Davies County.

Seeing Stanley smiling smugly, Hattie cringed. "Why on earth did Abner have to choose him as his best man?" Hattie, like most people, did not know of their long past together, and as she gave him the once over, she felt the same ominous feeling that she felt earlier. "I don't know why," she thought, "but I have a very bad feelin' about that man."

Knowing everyone was watching, Newton very gentlemanly gave Hattie to Abner. His phony behavior disgusted Hattie, and she watched begrudgingly as he and Jess retreated to their chairs in the front row. "The gall of those two," she thought angrily, "I hope you both get what you deserve." Exhaling heavily, she turned her attention to Reverend Walker and tried to appear content.

The Reverend, being Rebecca's confidant, knew that the marriage was only a matter of convenience and went along with it as a favor to her, however as a Minister, it bothered him deeply to know that this marriage was a mockery before God.

Chapter 4
THIRTY PIECES OF SILVER

LISTENING TO REVEREND WALKER administer the ceremony, Laville became lost in her thoughts. She didn't like thinking about her marriage to John Anderson, but after the confrontation she had with her mother, her mind just wouldn't put it to rest. Memories of a year ago came crashing down like a raging river over a waterfall. She hated to admit it, but her mother had been right, her marriage to John had been a tragedy. Still, she refused to accept the blame for what happened to John Anderson's parents, George and Emma. If it was anyone's fault, it was God's. After all, He let it happen.

She watched her Pa, as he slowly turned and glared at her. That hard disgruntled look that crossed his face was one she had seen far too many times in her life. Glaring back at him with the same intensity, she thought to herself, "You didn't win with me, Pa, and you'll not win with Hattie either." Then, smiling in a certain way that she knew only he understood (a perfect smile, one that hid pure hate), she recalled, all too well, her distasteful ordeal with him over John Anderson.

Her brothers, John and Robert, came home one evening and told her that they had overheard a conversation in the livery stable in Gallatin, between their Pa and George Anderson. They said they couldn't believe what they had heard, as their Pa was planning to marry off Laville to George's son, John. The 'thirty pieces of silver' Newton wanted in exchange for his daughter's hand in marriage was 300 acres of prime farmland that George owned. It lay south of the Morran farm, and was some of the best in the county. Newton insisted that it would be a fair trade. "After all, George," Newton said, "Laville *is* the most beautiful and most captivatin' woman in the state."

It was well known to the people of Gallatin that George and Emma Anderson were among the wealthiest landowners in the County. George had worked hard all his life and was an intelligent man. His hard work and good investments had paid off, and he and Emma now had a great deal of money, a mercantile business in Gallatin, and plenty of land.

Unfortunately, Emma Anderson, a delicate woman, had lost several children in childbirth, their son John being the only child to survive infancy. Because he was so cherished, he was given every advantage in life his well to do parents could afford, including the finest education in schools back East. He and Abner Garland had actually at one time attended the same school.

Though John had been pampered and often spoiled by his aging parents, he remained a good man. He was kind, loving, and totally devoted to his parents, and as a son, he made every effort to make them proud of him, never doing anything to embarrass or hurt them.

Laville, on the other hand, was extraordinarily beautiful, raven haired, olive skinned, and totally captivating. Like Delilah of old, she was highly intelligent, cunning, deceitful, and would lie at the drop of a hat if it served her purpose. As she grew into womanhood, she became sinfully provocative and manipulative, using her beauty to get what she wanted from the men around her. Even though she had made her family's life a living hell through her many escapades, when she was in trouble, they never failed to come to her aid.

John Anderson, like many other young men in Gallatin, had fallen in love with Laville. As far as he was concerned, she was the most beautiful woman in the world, and no matter how many other girls showed interest in him, he had his heart set on Laville. Because of his blind infatuation, he did everything in his power to win her heart, but alas, his efforts went unrewarded and his love unreturned.

Laville found John attractive and fun to tease, but certainly not interesting enough to pursue. She was holding out for the richest and most powerful man she could find, and would have considered Abner Garland herself, but she knew there was no way she could manipulate a man with as strong a will as his. It wasn't love she was looking for. "Who needs it?" she thought. An older man was what she wanted, one she could control with her sexual favors and still have affairs here and there if she wished. Long ago she had decided that it wasn't only money and position she wanted, but the power that great wealth could afford. Laville, unlike her siblings, embodied every selfish characteristic her father possessed and absolutely none of the characteristics of her angel-like mother.

In desperation, John Anderson finally went to his father, begging him to find a way to help make Laville his wife. George, who had always been able to use his money and power to get what he wanted, went straight to Newton to strike a devil's deal. Newton, being the greedy man he was, was more than willing to exchange

Laville for the land he wanted. After all, land meant an increase in position and power in the county, and Newton wanted those things, whatever the cost. The only thing George insisted on was that his son never find out about his deal with Newton. "My son is a proud man, Newt. It would kill him if he knew I had to purchase his wife."

After George and Newton agreed on their arrangement, Newton went to Laville, not knowing her brothers had told her of their conversation, and drove her some distance from the farm, where no one could hear their conversation. Before he could speak, Laville let him know she wanted no part of the deal.

"Damn it all, Laville, all you need to do is to stay married to John for a year, and I'll have 300 acres of the best land in the county. Then divorce him and you'll have all the money you want. Do this, and together, we'll outfox old George Anderson at his own game."

As she got out of the buggy and walked to a nearby stream, Laville strongly resisted. She hated her father, and for once, she was going to stand up to him regardless of the consequences. "And what if, God forbid, I should get pregnant during that time? The last thing in this world I want is a baby to drag around. To me, that would be a fate worse than death!" She paused before answering adamantly, "I just won't do it, Pa!"

Newton got out of the buggy, tied the horses up to a tree, and made his way to her. "Look, Laville, I know you've always wanted to get away from me." Pausing, he watched as she nodded weakly in agreement. "Well, here's your chance. But," his voice stopped as he moved in beside her and stroked her cheek lightly, "if you don't want to cooperate with me on this matter, thin's will go on between us just like they have all these years. In fact, no one's around, I don't see why we can't spend some time together right now." His eyes narrowed, as his hand slowly ran down her neck and settled on the top of her breast. He was so close that Laville could feel his hot breath on her face. She knew, all to well, what was about to happen.

Grabbing his hand and pushing him away, she tried in vain to control her anger. "How many times, since I was nine, have you forced me, Pa . . . thousands? Aren't you ever satisfied? Wasn't last night enough to last you a few days?" She was sick to death of him, and he was right, at this point she would do almost anything to get away from him. She started toward the buggy, but he quickly stepped in her way and grabbed her arm tightly. Realizing she lacked a way out of the situation, she conceded, "Oh, all right, Pa, I'll do it. I'll marry John Anderson; I'd marry the devil himself to get away from you!"

Satisfied, Newton let go of her arm but continued stroking it wantonly. "That's better; I knew you'd come to your senses." She glared at him and backed away, as he gave her a devilish smile. "Oh, and if it looks like young John isn't takin' care of your needs, I just might have to stop by when he's not at home and . . ." His voice trailed off, but he had gotten his point across.

Laville pulled away from him and started for the buggy again. "I told you, Pa, I would marry him, and you'll get the land you want. But that's all you'll ever get. I'm not putting up with your threats anymore."

Following Laville back to the buggy, Newton said, "John is comin' to the house tonight to officially ask me for your hand in marriage. His folks will be there later and, if you know what's good for you, you'll make sure they believe you're sincere about your love for him. If you don't, you'll have me to reckon with."

Laville got into the buggy. "Don't worry, Pa, I've been acting all my life, I know what to do. But you remember that when I marry John, everything stops between you and me." Untying the horses, Newton ignored her. "Look at me, Pa!" she screamed. "If I ever get the slightest hint that you've touched Hattie or Dakota, so help me God, even if I have to face being hanged, I'll chase you down like a dog in the street and shoot you!"

Newton took the reins, got in the buggy, and turned it around. "You do your part, that's all I care about." They rode several miles without speaking, then, stopping the buggy abruptly, he turned to her. "Better make sure your Ma believes you're in love with John, or she'll have no part in this. She ain't nobody's fool."

"Yes, Pa." Laville knew she had to make it look like she was cooperating, but she needed a plan of her own, some way to make sure she got everything she could out of this deal.

Twenty minutes later they pulled up in front of the house and found Minerva standing in the doorway. As Laville and Newton approached the house, they could see she was none too pleased. "Where in the dickens have you two been? We've been lookin' everywhere for the two of you."

"Taking a ride, Mama. I needed to talk to Pa about something."

Minerva frowned. "Like what? I've never known you two to talk about anythin'."

"John Anderson is coming over to talk to you and Pa this evening, Mama."

"What about?"

"He wants to marry me."

"What? I don't believe it. I know he likes you, Laville, but you've never paid one ounce of attention to him. Besides, you're not ready to get married."

"Now, Minerva, she's old enough," Newton protested.

Minerva, perplexed, gave Laville a suspicious look, then turned and entered the house. Laville shrugged her shoulders at her Pa, and he rolled his eyes. "She ain't goin' to be easy to convince, Laville," Newton said beneath his breath.

As Minerva busied herself making supper, she wondered, "Just what are they up to? There is somethin' fishy about all of this. Newton has never supported anyone unless it has served his own purpose. One thin' is for sure," she thought, "Puttin' those two together is like puttin' kerosene on a fire. Nothin' good can come from it."

Following supper that evening, Minerva heard a buggy pull up in front of the house. Looking at Laville, she said, "That must be John."

Having been assured by his Pa that Laville would accept his proposal of marriage, John arrived that evening quite confident. His parents, George and Emma, were to arrive an hour later.

While John and Laville went for a walk, Newton did his best to convince Minerva that John was definitely right for Laville.

"You're right, Newton, the boy has money behind him," Minerva agreed, "but why saddle such a nice boy with a girl like Laville, who has the temperament of a pit viper?"

"You're too hard on the girl, Minerva."

"Mark my words, Newt, nothin' good will come of this marriage. The boy is too good for Laville."

"Well, you know what I always say, if he ain't willin' to take the fall, he shouldn't take the ride. He's a smart young buck; I don't think Laville can outwit him."

"You underestimate your daughter, Newt. I love her, but I wouldn't trust her as far as I could throw her. It's obvious the two of you are goin' to do as you damn well please, just as you always do, but you leave me out of this. I'll have no part of this marriage."

After returning from their walk, Minerva listened intently to John, as he asked Newton for Laville's hand in marriage. Though he had come to the house on many occasions and took Laville for long walks and to church socials, Minerva had never seen the slightest spark of love for him in Laville's eyes.

George and Emma arrived promptly after the marriage proposal, and Emma was delighted that Laville had accepted John's proposal of marriage. Emma, a simple woman, had always believed Laville to be a vision of loveliness, and to think that she was actually going to be her daughter-in-law thrilled her. George, on the other hand, was worried because he knew of Laville's violent temper and strong will. But John's happiness was always his first concern, and if Laville was the girl he wanted to marry, than that was what he was going to get. All went well during the rest of the evening, as wedding arrangements between the two families were set and plans began to develop. With everyone agreeing that July 1st, 1895 would be the day of the ceremony, it seemed as though things were working out perfectly for John.

Laville couldn't have been sweeter to him, as she assured him that her Pa had convinced her that he would make a perfect husband. "Why, I'd be a fool to let a man like you get away, John." Kissing him tenderly and speaking like a perfect southern lady, she couldn't have given a more outstanding performance.

Through it all, John was totally unaware of the agreement between his father and Newton Morran. He honestly believed that

Laville wanted to marry him. He knew his father had been instrumental in the decision, but he didn't know how. John was so overwhelmed by Laville's beauty and so excited that she was willing to be his wife, he never questioned the honesty of the situation.

A month later, they were married as planned, and from the moment Laville said "I do", she set plans into motion to get even. With every beat of her heart, she vowed to outwit not only George and John Anderson, but her Pa as well. Whatever there was to gain from this marriage, it was going to be hers and hers alone. She didn't intend to lose anything, not even the original 300 acres struck in the deal between George and her Pa.

Immediately following her wedding ceremony, Laville turned and scanned her sea of guests. The first person that caught her eye was Ira Saxon, sitting next to his father Andrew. "John's not nearly as handsome as Ira," she thought, "and after I've got what I want from the Andersons, I'll have that good looking devil as well. He'll not turn me down; not when he sees I have money." Elated with her thoughts, she said to herself emphatically, "Yes! Yes! Yes! I'll have the Anderson fortune, and I'll have Ira Saxon, if it's the last thing I ever do!"

On their wedding night, Laville lay in John's arms and played the loving, adoring wife, smiling and whispering softly, "John, I'll love you forever." John, after having a taste of her, was completely mesmerized. He lost himself in every sensual curve of her body, as he took her over and over again. He, in his mind, had died and gone to heaven.

But, as fate would have it, 'forever' lasted only twelve days. The fantasy was shattered when John found her alone with Ira at a church picnic. First, he had seen Laville talking to Hattie, but then, a few minutes later, he saw her at the edge of the woods talking to Ira. Laville cleverly managed to draw Ira away from the picnic, and when John realized she was gone, he went looking for her. Searching feverishly, a wave of sickness passed over him. Quietly, he slipped away from the crowd and walked to the place he had last seen them. There he saw the lazy little path they had evidently strolled down, the one he knew led to the creek. Over and over the words came to him, "Oh, God, don't let me see something I don't want to see." His thoughts were frightening him, for he knew Ira was a handsome man and rumors were that he and Laville had once been lovers. Moments later, his suspicions were founded, as he saw the two of them standing together near the creek. He shielded himself from them by moving behind a few smaller trees.

Ira had his back to John, and Laville had her arms around his neck. Clearly John heard her begging Ira to slip away after the social, so they could be alone together. Immediately, his heart fell into the pit of his stomach, and he felt like he was going to be sick. But to his surprise, Ira defended him.

A tall, masculine man with piercing, brown eyes and dark brown hair, Ira spoke firmly. "Are you crazy, Laville? How do you think John would feel if he found you here alone like this with me? What's wrong with you? You know I'm not interested in you, yet you continue to try to seduce me. You're a married woman; isn't John enough of a man for you?"

Smiling slyly, she replied, "Well, he's certainly not the man you are, Ira, that's for sure. But, then again, few men are." With her tongue licking her lips seductively, she reached down, grabbed his manhood, and pulled him closer with her persuasive grip. "Compared to you, John's just a boy."

Disgusted with her games, Ira removed her arms from around his neck and pushed her away, "That's enough, Laville."

"What's the matter, Ira, afraid you'll fall in love with me . . . again?"

"Don't kid yourself, Laville. I might have thought I saw the promise of love in your eyes once, but through time, I've come to realize that it wasn't love at all, just lust. To tell you the truth, I don't think you're capable of lovin' anyone. You're too much in love with yourself." She drew back to slap him, but he caught her hand. "You'll have to find someone else to satisfy your lust, which will probably be pretty difficult, since you've bedded nearly every man in the county. But whatever you do, leave me alone. John Anderson is my friend, and I'll not betray him."

"Oh, don't be ridiculous, Ira, a little scampering around on the side isn't a betrayal."

"I really don't care what you call it, Laville; I'll have no part of it."

Sensing more drastic action was needed, she whirled around to face the creek and pretended as though she was about to cry. "Oh, Ira, I've never found another man like you. No one can light up my life like you do. When I'm in your arms, you make me forget there ever was another man."

"Cut the theatrics, Laville. It won't work. You walked off and left me as if I meant nothin' a long time ago. I thought of you every day and dreamed of you every night. I've never felt such heartache, and I promised myself that I'd never put myself through that again." Taking her arm, he gently turned her around. Her eyes, face, and lips were so beautiful that for a moment he was afraid he would succumb. Then, remembering again what she had put him through, he gained the strength he needed and gazed back at her with determination. "You are definitely beautiful, Laville. I'd say you're probably the most beautiful woman I have ever known, but you can't be trusted. If you can't be true to John, as good a man as he is, I know that you'd never be true to me."

Breathlessly, she murmured, "We were lovers once, Ira, and we can be again. One day I'll have all the money I could ever want, and together, we can get away from this dreadful place."

John stood broken-hearted and furious all at the same time, as he watched his wife, who had made love to him just the night before, taunting, pleading, and practically throwing herself at his friend. Stepping into the clearing, he took several steps in their direction and small twigs crackled beneath his feet. Laville, seeing that it was John, raced toward him, crying out that Ira had led her there to seduce her. Pulling her hands from about his neck as Ira had done, he pushed her away. Looking at her in disgust and overcome with grief, he began to cry. "I've stood here, Laville, and heard every word. I'll not listen to your lies another minute."

Turning to Ira, he said weakly, "Thank you for not betraying our friendship."

Ira nodded. "I couldn't, John. We've been friends too long."

Turning around, John walked away. Hot tears ran down his face as he said to himself, "How could I have been such a fool?" Vivid memories of her lying breathless in his arms raced frantically through his mind. The sound of her screaming out his name in ecstasy rang in his ears with the force of a thousand church bells. Her soft loving words, her seductive stares, and her voluptuous body had completely devoured him. And now, the love that he thought was so real, so pure, and so true was cutting at his heart like a knife.

From behind him, he could hear Laville calling, "John, come

back! Please, Darling, don't leave; let me explain!" He ignored her pleas, as he kept on walking, tears running down his face.

That night at supper both Laville and John hid behind masks of tragedy, as they ate supper with his parents at their farmhouse, and then, at ten o'clock, they retired as usual. Closing the bedroom door behind him, he felt Laville's seductive touch, running her hands up and down his back, teasing him. "Do you forgive me, Darling?"

Appalled that she even mentioned forgiveness, John turned around, faced her, and yelled, "No, Laville, it's over! Even if I wanted to, I could never forgive you for what you did to me today! You have wrecked me in every way possible! Every word, every kiss, every touch, it was all a lie!" Shaking his head in disgust, he continued, "We will live in this house and in this bedroom together until I can figure out what I'm going to do, but our marriage from this point on is over. I can't trust you, and I can't allow myself to be hurt any more than I am now."

Moving in closer, she spoke with a spiteful tone, as she provocatively played with her nightshirt. "You'll not do a damn thing, my dear Jonathan, for fear of hurting your adoring parents, George and Emma." Her words cut like a double-edged sword.

"You're right, I'll not have them hurt the way you've hurt me. You sleep in the bed, and I'll sleep on the floor. But believe me when I say, I'll not have anything else to do with you ever again."

After several weeks and after every attempt to tantalize him into her bed had failed, Laville announced over supper one evening that she was going to have John's baby. Emma and George were ecstatic at the news and immediately started making plans, as Laville was going to give them the one thing in the world they had wanted most, a grandchild.

John, shocked and enraged, left the house that night, walked for hours, and didn't return until morning. He couldn't believe Laville would make up such a lie. The next day when his folks went into Gallatin, he stormed into the parlor and confronted her. "How dare you tell my parents a lie like that?"

"A lie!" In anger, she drew back and slapped him. "It wouldn't be a lie if you acted like a real man and slept with me." Slapping him a second time, she continued, "If you were a real man like Ira, I would be pregnant, John."

"Keep your hateful remarks to yourself, Laville. You're not going to goad me into anything; those days are over. Do whatever the hell you want. As for me, I'm leaving tonight and I'm not coming back until you're gone." Quickly, he left the room and went to their bedroom, where he took out a satchel and began putting clothes in it.

Laville was furious. Following him to their room, she went to the bed where his clothes were laying, grabbed them in her arms, went to the window, and threw them out onto the ground. "There, you Bastard, they're lying in the dirt right where you ought to be. Get out and don't worry about coming back, because, Honey, I'm not leaving! Wild horses couldn't drag me away from this farm and your parents' money!"

Storming out of the room, he yelled, "Pregnant, ha! I ought to wring your pretty little neck! How are you going to lie your way out of this one?"

Running after him, she yelled, "That's none of your affair, John. Just take your clothes and get out. And, as for wringing my pretty neck, I think you got the wrong person. You ought to wring your Pa's neck. I only married you because he and my Pa struck a deal.

Newton got some of that precious farm land of yours in exchange for me!" Hearing the truth about his marriage was the final blow. John left his parents' house a broken man, with his head hung down in shame, never to return.

Under normal circumstances, Laville's plan would have taken many months, if not years, to carry out, but thanks to John's leaving, she knew that by the end of her supposed pregnancy, she would have everything she had ever wanted. The greatest lie of her life was now destined to unfold in all its horrendous glory. The following morning she arose early, and crying crocodile tears, she ran to George and Emma's bedroom. Throwing herself into Emma's arms, she sobbed that she had awakened to find an empty bed and a note from John. It read, "I'm tired living a lie, Laville. I'm in love with another woman. I only married you to please my parents. I'm sorry. I know I've hurt you." Laville acted out her part perfectly, as she cried, "Oh, Mother Anderson, what did I do wrong?"

Unbeknownst to the Andersons, Laville had written the note herself. The Anderson's couldn't tell the difference because Laville was an excellent forger. As a young girl, she realized she had a gift. She could look at a person's handwriting and, with a little practice, could duplicate it so well that even the person whose signature she forged couldn't tell the difference.

At first Emma could hardly believe the note, but as she read it over and over and with it appearing to be in her son's own handwriting, she finally succumbed. A week later, Laville searched until she found a young woman in a nearby County who would cooperate with her and paid her to play the other woman. According to Laville's perfect plan, the woman arrived late one evening, asking for John's personal things and had another note for Emma, which

Laville had also forged. The note simply stated that John would never return, as he had found out that Laville had been forced into the marriage to him. When Emma read George this new letter, he tearfully admitted the truth and said that he thought he was doing the right thing for John's sake. With Emma utterly devastated, Laville played it for all it was worth. In the days that followed, she pretended to fall ill and Emma, fearing Laville might miscarry, put her to bed. Pretending to be heartbroken, Laville told George and Emma that she was a woman scorned and had no other choice but to divorce John and return home to her family.

Emma loved Laville and couldn't stand the thought of losing not only John but Laville as well, along with the supposed unborn grandchild. She had to do something. She couldn't stand the thought of her family falling apart right before her eyes. Calling on the Sheriff to help, she made every effort to find John. Finally finding him in a little town in Illinois, she wrote a letter to John begging him to return home to them and Laville.

John, totally unaware of the diabolical scheme Laville had set in motion during his absence, replied in just one word, "No."

With John's response, George and Emma were convinced that everything Laville had presented was true, and her evil plans fell even more perfectly into place. The Andersons were playing right into her hands. They were so desperate to hang onto her that they were willing to do anything in their power to convince her to remain with them, which was exactly what she had planned all along. Being the charlatan that she was, Laville convinced Emma and George to make all their assets at the bank available to her, so that she could join Emma in their mercantile business in Gallatin. George, disappointed in John beyond reason, fell into Laville's scheming hands like a lamb being led to the slaughter.

The Anderson's mercantile store in Gallatin was very successful, and the thought of having Laville with her all the time was exciting for Emma. Laville marched right in on a grand scale, updating the store and remodeling the building. After all, Gallatin was a growing city, and she insisted George mustn't let anyone outdo him. Watching Laville work wonders for their business, George and Emma were mesmerized with her ability to not only work with people, but they also admired her flair for business. It had been their plan that John would have taken over the business, but they were grateful, now, that it was Laville.

Realizing that time was against her, Laville placed a small pillow beneath her dress to make her supposed pregnancy appear real. As time progressed, so did the size of the pillow. When she looked too far along to appear in public, she remained in the office on the second floor of the mercantile store, immersing herself in the books on George's business. Even though Laville didn't have much of a formal education, she had an uncanny ability to cipher and could read and write extremely well. Being highly intelligent, she was starved for knowledge, and as a child, she had insisted that her Uncle Paul's limited library be left in her parent's home, where she and Hattie could read and study. Their Pa had made fun of them, saying, "Women don't need any book learnin'," but Laville was undaunted. She studied as much as time would allow, and even from an early age, she tried to act like a real lady, going to great lengths to speak and act correctly. Given her extensive knowledge on so many different subjects coupled with her new-found business savvy, Laville had all the tools necessary to make her plan successful.

Near the end of her supposed pregnancy, Laville set the final stages of her plan in motion. She sent George and Emma on a buying trip for the store, and as soon as they were gone, she presented deeds with forged signatures to the Court House for recording, giving not only their farm but also the store and other holdings in town to her and John. The forged signatures were witnessed by two men she had seen come to the farm asking for a loan which George had refused. Knowing the men were desperate for money, Laville offered them the loan herself providing that they witness the signatures she had forged. Within days, she began taking substantial amounts of money from the Anderson account at the bank and placed it in her name in a Bank in Iowa.

Knowing exactly where John was from the Sheriff, Laville invited three unsavory men to the farm and hired them to travel to Illinois and engage John in a card game. At first it wasn't clear what it was she wanted them to do. "I don't want to be part of any guessin' game, Mrs. Anderson," one of them stated. "Do you want him discredited, embarrassed, or what?"

 Leaning against the mantle of the fireplace and placing her hand beneath her hair, she swept it all forward to one side and over her shoulder in one dramatic gesture. Then, her eyes narrowed, as she spoke in a deep throaty voice. "I want him dead. Is that plain enough? And," she said with a pause, "I don't want to know when or how," she said coldly. "Just do it quickly, and make damn sure it will look like self-defense to the law. You'll have your money when I get word from the Sheriff here in Gallatin that the sorry little bastard is dead!"

The men left the farm in the dark of night and two days later John Anderson was dead. Sheriff Sanders, knowing that George and Emma were out of town, took his wife and rode out to the Anderson farm late that evening to break the news to Laville. Laville pretended to faint when Sheriff Sanders told her John had been killed, in what was called by the local authorities as a scuffle during a card game. "I was told," the Sheriff said, "that he got all liquored up and drew on some men, Miss Laville, and they shot him in self-defense."

Laville told the Sheriff where to reach George and Emma, so he could wire them of John's death. They returned home several days later overwhelmed with grief. At the funeral, Laville did her best to stand between the Andersons and every person who came to offer their condolences. But somehow to her dismay, the banker got past her. And, as she turned to leave, she saw him talking to George. Suddenly, the expression on George's face changed, and he looked directly at her. His expression told her that he knew she had taken almost all of their money.

"Damn!" she thought. "He's found out too soon. What am I going to do now?"

George could hardly believe what the banker had told him. It seemed unthinkable to him that Laville had taken nearly everything they owned. Now, not only had they lost John, but they were nearly penniless as well. His grief over the death of John and the shock of finding out what Laville had done had George in a rage when he reached the farm. Finding Laville alone in the parlor and knowing that Emma had remained behind at the Cemetery, he confronted her. "I demand you return my money, Laville!"

She refused.

"Why on Earth would you do this to Emma and me? All we've ever done is love you and treat you like a daughter."

"Because I hate you, George, for what you and my Pa did in forcing me to marry John in the first place. After what you put me through, old man, I'd just as soon see you begging on the streets of Gallatin, as give you one bite of food from 'my' kitchen!" Shaking her fist at him, she screamed, "You and Pa just make me sick. What in the world ever made you think that I'd go along with you, like a lamb to the slaughter? If you thought that I would stay with your precious little Johnny boy and raise a house full of snotty nosed kids, you're sadly mistaken. That was the last thing in this world I would ever do!"

"How in the hell did you get to my money?"

"That was easy the easy part, but it's not only money. I've taken this farm, the store, and all the rest of your holdings as well."

Sitting down behind his desk, George buried his face in his hands. "You're certainly not the same young woman we grew to love and trust." Looking up, he saw her face full of spite. "How could you do this, Laville? Have you no shame?"

"Not an ounce. Shame is not a part of my vocabulary. If you had gone through anywhere near the horror of what I've went through in my life, you wouldn't have any shame either."

Again he begged her, "Please give me back what's rightfully mine. Didn't you know that everything we have would have been yours? I thought that your marrying John would give you a far better chance than you had on your Pa's farm, and honestly, I thought John loved you. He told me over and over and over again that he wanted to marry you. I still find it hard to believe he was in love with someone else."

"Well, your precious little John is gone now, I saw to that. I took your money, your property, and your dignity. You have nothing left, which is what I had planned the whole time. No one plays Laville Morran Anderson for a fool and gets away with it. You entered into an evil bargain with my Pa, and now you're paying the price. Deal with it."

As Laville backed several steps across the room toward the door to leave, George became so enraged that he reached in his desk drawer and pulled out his revolver. Realizing the depth of evil that consumed Laville and knowing he'd never get his money back, he aimed the revolver at her. Like a man possessed, he yelled, "Damn you, Laville, you've stolen everything from me, and if you won't give me back what's mine then I'm going to send you square to hell where you belong!" Emma, who had arrived home sooner than George had thought, heard shouting and entered the room just as George was about to shoot. Looking upon the scene, she thought that George had lost his mind. Not knowing that Laville had stolen anything and loving her as she did, Emma leaped in front of Laville, screaming, "No, George, No!", just as the gun was fired. The gunshot echoed through the small farmhouse like a clap of thunder, and Emma was shoved back by the force of the blast. Falling into Laville's arms, they fell to the floor in a heap. A second later, a faint trace of blood showed through the delicate fabric of Emma's dress. She had been hit. Laville never dreamed her scheme and lies would come to this, and as she gazed into Emma's pale face, it was obvious she was dying.

George cried out in horror, "Oh, My God! What have I done?"

Laville screamed across the room at him, "She's dead, you fool! You've killed her!"

With his hands shaking violently and his sobbing uncontrollable, he raised the gun to his head and cried, "Oh God, forgive me. I've killed my precious Emma." The sound of the second gunshot echoed eerily throughout the room, nearly sending Laville into shock. So much so, that she couldn't utter a sound.

Emma, not understanding what had occurred between George

and Laville, feebly reached up and touched Laville's face. A moment later, her eyes closed and her hand fell across her chest. Laville sat stunned, holding Emma's lifeless body in her arms. It was then Laville realized that she couldn't hear anything. The sound of the gun having been fired twice, only moments apart, had left her temporarily deaf.

Looking around the room in disbelief, Laville couldn't help but run the traumatic events of the past few minutes over and over in her mind. In less than a heartbeat, both George and Emma were dead. She kept thinking to herself, "This wasn't the way it was supposed to have ended." No matter how diabolical her actions had been up to this point, Laville had never intended for them to die, but what was done was done. So, with the reality of the situation setting in and with satisfaction that she had taken from George what she felt he owed her, Laville leaned back against the wall and waited for the farm hands to arrive.

Hearing the screams and gunshots, the hired hands ran to the house. Opening the door, they were shocked by the horrific scene before them. Laville moaned as Chester Wright, the main farm hand, reached down and took Emma's lifeless body from her, then lifted Laville into his arms.

"For Heaven's sake, Miss Laville, what happened?" he asked.

Still unable to hear well, she mumbled, "Send someone for the Sheriff and my Mama, Chester. George went crazy, killed Emma, and took his own life. I think he intended to kill me, too." Then, pretending, she fainted.

In the minutes that followed, Chester found it impossible to gain control of himself. He had worked for the Andersons for the past twenty years and loved them as family. "Wake up, Miss Laville, wake up," he said, trying to awaken her, as he carried her from the room.

Later that day, Laville had no difficulty convincing Sheriff Sanders and his wife that George, thinking all was lost in losing John, had lost his mind, killed Emma, and then himself. The Sheriff had no reason to believe any different, as all the evidence supported her.

Before the inquest was held over George's and Emma's deaths, Laville went over and over what she would tell the authorities. All she had to do was convince them, and her evil plan would be complete. The story she told the authorities was that John and Emma had been deeply concerned about George's mental condition for some time. In desperation, they had George sign over the farm and store to John and herself, before John left. Then, Emma took George on their buying trip, and John had asked Laville to take the money from the bank in Gallatin and have it deposited in an Iowa bank in her name. By doing so, his father could not, in his mental state, lose the family fortune. Finally, she said that she had been in contact with an asylum at the Capitol just in case George's condition worsened, and she paid off a secretary at the asylum to back up her story.

Everything held up at the inquest because there wasn't a living soul to contest it, and after what had occurred, it appeared to be the complete truth. Laville put on quite a performance, crying and fainting during the questioning. She pleaded with the Judge, asking him to not divulge what she had said to the public. After all, John and Emma had gone to great lengths to keep George's mental condition a secret. "Now," she pleaded, "I'm afraid it will all be exposed."

Poor Laville gained the sympathy of the entire town because

she was so convincing. Neither Sheriff Sanders, nor anyone else, questioned her truthfulness. After all, this raving beauty was suffering deeply, having lost her husband and both her in-laws, and appearing great with child. She was the only surviving member of the Anderson family, and everyone felt she was entitled to everything the Andersons had accumulated.

Planning well, Laville had left no stone unturned. She knew exactly what to say and how to say it.

The whole community was moved emotionally, as it looked as though the birth of her child was all that Laville had left in life. Waiting patiently until her Mother, Dakota, and Hattie went out of town for a weekend, Laville planned her last move, and while they were gone, pretended to have a miscarriage. Her lie was supported by a friend, and when the women returned, there was a fourth grave in the Anderson family cemetery, for her supposed child.

Walking away from the grave sight, Minerva said under her breath, "I've half a mind to come back here tonight and dig up that grave."

"Mama," Hattie responded in horror, "you can't mean that?"

"Oh, yes, I do. I'll bet you even money, there's nothin' there but an empty coffin."

"Just let it be, Mama. I'd be afraid we'd be struck down by a bolt of lightnin' if we open that grave." Even though Minerva never believed Laville's story, the grave was left undisturbed, its secret never known.

The preacher's wife, Martha Walker, and many other good women of the church stayed with Laville daily, as she supposedly recovered. Every woman in town felt that Laville was truly a saint among women. In one month's time, it seemed this 'Joan of Arc', as she became known, had endured every heartache imaginable.

Satan, Laville's cohort, smiled, as he watched her end up with exactly what she had wanted. By scheming, conniving, and lying, she had beat George, her Pa, and John, ending up with everything. And now that she had a taste of what a lot of money could do for her, she would never again be the same.

Chapter 5
FOR GOD SHALL NOT BE MOCKED

REALIZING SHE'D BEEN DAYDREAMING for quite some time, Laville focused her attention back on the wedding. Several minutes passed and she couldn't shake the feeling that someone was watching her. Turning, she scanned those sitting behind her and saw Ira Saxon sitting between his father, Andrew, and his sister, Emily. Whispering to herself, she said, "How dare he show his face here after all the misery he caused me?"

"Pay attention, Laville," Robert said, nudging her.

Looking forward, she heard the preacher ask, "If anyone has any reason why these two should not be joined together in holy matrimony, let him speak now or forever hold his peace." Again she turned in Ira's direction. Glaring at him with contempt, as he hung his head listening to the ceremony, Laville vowed to get even with him for refusing her.

At that same moment, Hattie glanced out into her great sea of guests. Her eyes quickly caught Andrew's, and beside him, she saw Ira with his head bowed. "What must Ira think of me?" she thought.

Raising his head, Ira saw Hattie looking in his direction.

Glancing around carefully to see if anyone was watching him and feeling that there wasn't, he said silently with his lips, "I love you."

Hattie's heart leapt at Ira's silent token, and if only for a moment, Hattie felt like things were somehow going to work themselves out.

Abner, perturbed that Hattie wasn't paying attention to him, gave her hand a hard tight squeeze. The preacher paused, grateful that this ordeal was nearly over, and then stated, "That which God has joined together this day, let no man put asunder."

A chill ran up Hattie's spine, as she looked into Abner's eyes and saw a devilish smile cross his face. Silently she heard in her mind the words repeated, "For God shall not be mocked," broken by Reverend Walker's words, "You may now kiss your bride, Abner."

As Abner lifted her veil, Hattie stood motionless, looking up into his cold, calculating eyes. She forced a smile and, muttering under her breath, said, "I'd rather be kissin' a rattlesnake."

Tossing her veil lightly over her head, Abner replied just as quietly. "Believe me, by the time I get even with you, you'll wish you were." With that statement, he pulled Hattie to him so tight that she could hardly breathe and kissed her mouth as hard as he could. As he did, she bit his lip and shoved the revolver in her bouquet into his chest. Feeling the hard steel, he released her and they turned once again to face Reverend Walker. Still whispering, Abner said, "I *will* get even with you, Miss Hattie Garland, for everything you've taken from me, if it's the last thing I ever do."

Reverend Walker, hearing everything, sighed deeply and turned his eyes heavenward. Seeing his reaction, Hattie tried to comfort the Minister, whispering, "You did the best you could, Reverend, I promise you, you'll not be held accountable." Hoping that the

Reverend took her words to heart, Hattie turned around and faced her guests. It was show time. She smiled an effervescent smile and said brightly, "Ladies and Gentlemen, we're so happy to have you here with us today. Allow me to introduce ourselves. We are Mr. and Mrs. Abner Garland of Gallatin, Missouri. Welcome to our home." Then, just as she finished speaking, she whirled around like Cinderella and curtsied deeply, totally mesmerizing the crowd.

Almost immediately, a thunderous applause broke out among the guests. Laville, hearing it, yanked on Robert's arm. "How dramatic!" she cooed. "Why didn't I think of that at my wedding?"

"Face it, Laville," he said over the noise of the crowd, "she's got you outclassed and probably always will."

As the roar of the crowd continued ringing loudly in Laville's ears, she, for a short moment, though she felt one of her excruciating headaches coming on. They were the kind which caused her to black out, and in her mind, she cried out, "Oh, no, please God, not now, please!" Great beads of perspiration formed on her brow, and taking her handkerchief, she blotted her face lightly, while smiling weakly at her brother, John, who was seated behind her.

The reception was a complete success, as everything worked out just as Rebecca and Minerva had planned. After the wedding, all of the chairs were swiftly cleared to the exterior of the court by Rebecca's hired hands to allow for maximum reception space. Hattie and her family were known throughout the area for their singing, and halfway into the afternoon, Rebecca made a special announcement. "Hattie is going to sing a new song that she has written especially for this occasion. It is all about her love for Abner."

Making her way with Abner to a makeshift stage off to the side of the veranda where the orchestra was located, Hattie smiled and waved to her guests. She had written the song all right, but with Ira Saxon in mind, not Abner. It didn't matter, though, as the song would serve her purpose.

Because the stage area was even with the height of the veranda, the new bride and groom could be viewed easily not only by the immense crowd in the court but also by those sitting at the tables on the veranda. As they stepped onto the stage, a chair was brought to Abner, and he was invited by Hattie to sit down. Singing as soft and sweet as a nightingale, she walked around him, in what appeared to be complete adoration.

Hattie was nobody's fool. She had learned a lot about showmanship from her Uncle Paul, who himself was quite a showman. Through his tutoring, she had acquired the skills to captivate and hold an audience emotionally. Abner, of course, enjoyed being the center of attention and, as much as he hated to admit it, he was completely spellbound by Hattie's voice. The words were romantic and the sound enchanting. Her lovely soprano voice carried the melody perfectly, as her family, sounding like a church choir, sang the backup vocals perfectly. Their strong voices carried beautifully from where they were standing off in the background, and the crowd hung on Hattie's every word.

For years "The Singing Morrans," as they were known, had been entertaining at Church socials and county fairs and had earned themselves quite a reputation. As she was ending her song, Hattie led Abner to a circular portion of the stage platform that was specifically built for her song. As they stepped on it, that area began to revolve, and slowly, they turned like two porcelain figurines on a music box, as the song came to its dramatic end. The effect was exactly what Rebecca had hoped, breathtaking. Her family applauded enthusiastically, followed instantaneously by the guests, who were still mesmerized. As Hattie curtsied delicately, the Governor and his wife moved forward through the applauding crowd to meet Abner's incredible young bride. Taking Hattie's hands in his and speaking to Abner, he exclaimed, "What a prize you've found yourself, Abner! You needn't worry about having to run a campaign, just let this little lady sing your way right into the Governor's Mansion." Abner stood with pride, as if he were personally responsible for the presentation. He hated Hattie for what she and his mother had done to him, but he was so hungry for the power that politics could afford him that he would use any tactic necessary to impress the powers that be. And right now, whether he liked it or not, Hattie was it.

During the remainder of the afternoon, many of the guests made it a point to mention to Abner that he was a lucky man to have an angel of a wife like the young, beautiful, and talented "Miss Hattie." Through it all, the thought kept occurring to her, "I can't believe I'm doin' this. I can't believe I'm actually married to this snake." Sensing her feelings, Rebecca kept reassuring Hattie throughout the reception, "I give you my solemn promise, my dear, this will all be worth it."

By late in the afternoon, Laville noticed her Pa and Jess were drinking heavily. Worriedly, she watched as her mother tried to discourage Newton from drinking any more. Knowing her mother would stand no match against Newton if he should get out of hand, Laville hastily made her way to her older brothers, who were visiting with friends out by the gazebo in the gardens. Reaching them, she informed them of the situation. "Pa's over by the bar and he's starting to cause trouble. I suggest the three of you get over there soon because Ma can only contain him so long."

Without another word Shannon, Robert, and John made their way back through the gardens along with five of their friends. Walking together side by side, they looked very formidable. They were all hard-working farm boys and their well-defined physiques showed through the handsome black suits they were wearing. As they approached the scene, they heard Minerva swear at her husband. "Damn it, Newton, I said get your no good drunken ass out of here. I'll not let you make a scene and ruin what Rebecca and I have worked so hard to create."

The boys were caught aback as they rarely ever heard Minerva swear except for extreme circumstances, but they knew even though she was a dainty woman, she could be a spitfire when you made her angry. Newton, however, wasn't threatened in the least and in his anger drew back to slap Minerva for insulting him, but before his hand could land on its intended target, Shannon caught his arm in midair. He, along with his brothers and friends, then proceeded to easily pick Newton completely off the ground, secure him so that he couldn't move or talk, and carry him inconspicuously away from the reception. The Morran brothers returned to the reception rather quickly but left their five friends to watch their father. Shannon left instructions for them to use whatever force necessary to make sure Newton did not return, and rumor had it days later that Newton had some pretty good bruises on his face.

With tragedy averted, Laville and Minerva made their way to Rebecca and Hattie and told them about what had just happened. Together, they hoped the whole scene had gone unnoticed by the guests.

Rebecca, seeing Shannon returning, reassured them, "It appears to me that your brothers have everything under control." Turning to Hattie, she continued, "Come now, Dear, let's take Abner and visit with the Governor's party." Hattie looked nervously toward her mother, who acknowledged that everything was indeed okay and that she should go.

Hattie had been unsure about her ability to mix in social gatherings of high society, until Rebecca spent many hours during the past two months grooming her on proper etiquette. Now, all that hard work was going to pay off. She waited for just the right moment then asked shyly, "So, do you believe this wonderful husband of mine has a place in politics, Governor?"

He smiled. "Oh, my yes, Young Lady. With his education, good looks, and his mother's fortune, along with your support, he can't lose."

Abner tried to seize the moment and to take over the conversation, but Hattie wouldn't let him. She did just as she had said she would, she charmed the pants off the Governor and his party, and in spite of the fact that he couldn't get a word in edgewise, Abner was pleased.

The Governor's wife, noticing Hattie was still holding her bouquet, asked if she intended to toss it, as was the tradition. Hattie winked at Abner and holding it closer replied, "Oh, I would, Ma'am, but my sister Laville made this, and I just can't bear to part with it."

The Governor, not only enchanted with Hattie's beauty and poise, but also her sweetness, said, "So, Little Lady, would you like to live in the Governor's Mansion? As we see it, there's a real chance that your husband will become the Governor of the State of Missouri one day."

"Governor, is your mansion as beautiful as this one?"

Smiling sheepishly, he answered, "Oh, my heavens, no. This is without a doubt the most elegant home in the state."

"Well, then may I say somethin' for the record, as we have so many gentlemen from the Press here today?" She paused to formulate the right words in her mind. "The people of this State have no idea what would be in store for them, if my Abner ever held your office." She made it sound as if it was a compliment, but Abner wasn't fooled. He knew exactly what she meant.

Being interested in this talented and rare beauty, the Governor's wife asked, "Miss Hattie, I've heard you are lady of many talents. According to those I've talked to, you have written a number of songs including the one you sang earlier, are a very accomplished artist, and to top it all off, rumor is you are an excellent marksman with a pistol and a rifle. Is all of this true, my dear?"

Before Hattie could answer, Rebecca took over the conversation. She beamed with pride, as she began talking to the Governor's party. "You'll find that my darling new daughter-in-law is quite modest. Luckily, her new mother doesn't have that problem. It is a well-known fact that Hattie is an excellent shot. Hattie's ability to shoot is so good, in fact, that she has been compared to none other than the infamous Annie Oakley. As far as I know, Miss Hattie seldom misses her target and can hit her mark even while standing on a horse's back at a full gallop. She has won every exhibition she has ever entered and even traveled for a season with a circus with her uncle, Paul Moore, who is a well-known trick shooter."

The Governor was thoroughly impressed and decided to extend an invitation to this intriguing young couple. "You and Abner must come to the Capitol, Miss Hattie, and be our guests."

Before Hattie could answer, Abner, realizing he had lost the spotlight to his multi-talented new bride, suggested they mingle among some other prominent guests. Excusing himself and Hattie, they left the Governor's party.

As Rebecca had taught, Hattie made it a point to speak to everyone, charming all with her undivided attention. Strolling through the gardens of Silver Creek, they were a handsome couple. Abner towered over Hattie's petite frame, his ruddy dark complexion complimented the ivory softness of her skin, and her auburn red hair and green eyes accentuated the black in his hair and the dark blue in his eyes. As they passed by, several lady friends of Rebecca commented to her, "No doubt, Rebecca, that they will have beautiful children."

Abner, enthralled with the amount of important people at the reception, was having the time of his life. He was taking advantage of every opportunity to enhance his self-image by rubbing shoulders with the crème de la crème of Missouri society. Fortunately for Hattie, this obsession of his allowed her to slip away. Abner was so engrossed with the congressman he was talking to that he didn't even notice she had left, and she immediately crossed the court to the veranda where Dakota, James, and the Saxon family were sitting around a table visiting. Emily, who was Ira's older sister, greeted her with a warm embrace. Whispering quietly, she said, "James explained everythin' to us, so we understand what's goin' on. We're all worried sick about you, Miss Hattie. You better be careful; Abner can be a very dangerous man."

As Hattie let go of Emily, Andrew Saxon, Ira's father, reached out to her. His eyes, once a brilliant blue, were now dimmed with old age and ill health. "How are you holdin' up, my Dear?" he asked.

"Better than I expected. I'm so sorry I haven't been in closer touch with you, Mr. Saxon, but since this all began, I've not been able to get away from the estate, even once. Rebecca said Abner and Jess would have men watchin' me."

Speaking softly, Emily said, "Ira was in Kansas City until three days ago when he got Papa's telegram. At first, he couldn't understand what was goin' on, and neither could we. James Kinnion finally came to the farm yesterday and told us that you had sent many letters to Ira, but evidently they were intercepted, most likely by your Pa."

Rolling her eyes, Hattie hated her father interfering in everything. "I'm sure he did, Emily. He'd do anythin' to keep me from ruinin' his plans." Turning to Ira, she asked shamefully, "What must you have thought of me, Ira?"

"I didn't know what to think. Last summer at the fair, you said you would wait for me. The next thin' I knew, I saw an article in the newspaper that announced your impendin' marriage to Abner Garland. That was the same day I got a telegram from Pa. Accordin' to Pa's instructions, I got on the first train back to Gallatin, but for the life of me, I couldn't understand why you would be marryin' anyone, let alone the likes of Abner. I still didn't understand until James told us Rebecca had pleaded with you to marry Abner, so that she could give you her fortune."

Looking to see if Abner was still talking with the Senator, Hattie was pleased with what she saw, as he was not only still talking to the congressman but also a slew of other state politicians. Feeling safe that Abner wouldn't be looking for her, Hattie turned back to face Ira. She grabbed hold of his hands and spoke as sincerely as she could. "It's true, Ira, every word. Rebecca has made me the wealthiest young woman in the country. And once the dust settles on this marriage, we will finally be able to be together." Smiling, Ira pulled Hattie close, embracing her, and for one small moment, Hattie felt that everything would work out.

Andrew, even though he was glad to see Ira and Hattie resolving the confusion that had been between them, still had other questions he wanted answered. "Tell me, Miss Hattie, how is your Mama? The latest scuttlebutt around Gallatin has it that she's left your Pa."

"It's true, she has," Hattie replied. "She brought Dakota and the boys and moved into the mansion three days after I did. I wish I could keep things quiet, especially from the waggin' tongues around here. The press is bad enough around Rebecca with her being such a prominent figure of High Society and all, but the local gossips in Gallatin can have every move we make spread all over town, long before the newspapers ever know."

Emily sighed. "It's a cryin' shame your Mama has to resort to divorce, but your Pa has mistreated her for so long. I surely can't blame her." Letting out a deep breath, she continued, "Knowin' Abner like I do, I'm really curious as to how you are goin' to keep him from gettin' his mangy hands on his mother's fortune now that you're married to him?"

James, who had been sitting silently, spoke up so that everyone could hear. "I can answer that, Emily. I drew up the divorce papers and witnessed the signatures. The night Rebecca and Hattie confronted Abner and Jess, she forced them to sign a number of documents, including the divorce papers. They had no choice, as Judge Stepp, Sheriff Sanders, and I were all present. Believe me when I say that the threat against Hattie and her family was only the tip of the iceberg concerning the Garlands. Rebecca's private investigator had accumulated enough evidence on Jess and Abner to have them put in prison for a very long time. Judge Stepp, Sheriff Sanders, and

Reverend Walker have been fully aware of this whole sordid mess from the very beginning, and were in full cooperation with Rebecca. Believe me, neither Abner nor Jess has a leg to stand on."

Hattie, wanting again to reassure Ira and his family that things would work out, said sweetly, "I want all of you to remember, Rebecca will be insistin' that both Jess and Abner leave shortly after the reception. This is a marriage in name only and will never be consummated."

Andrew, in awe of Hattie's poise under pressure, gave her a quick smile. "It took a pretty brave woman to go through all this, Miss Hattie."

"Not brave, Mr. Saxon, more like desperate. Our family needed to get away from Pa, and this was the only way out."

Andrew nodded his head solemnly in agreement, as he had never liked Newton Morran. Unbeknownst to everyone present, Andrew knew exactly what type of man Newton was and just what he was capable of. He liked Minerva and the kids, though, and felt for them in their current situation. "Hattie," Andrew said quite suddenly, as if he had just remembered something. "Do you ever remember Newton havin' business contacts North of here in Iowa or Minnesota because when I ran into him a couple weeks ago he said he was headed North on business?"

Hattie shrugged her shoulders indicating she didn't know but then paused as she thought about the subject before answering. "To be honest with you, Mr. Saxon, Pa has always been strange like that. Before we left the farm, it was not uncommon for him to leave for months at a time to tend to business issues. At first I thought it was strange, but as I grew older, I just learned to accept it. Besides, at least when he was gone, he couldn't mistreat us." As Hattie completed her sentence, she hung her head slightly and tried to push the thoughts of her Pa's meanness out of her mind.

Cody, sensing Hattie needed a pick-me-up, took her hand and squeezed it three times, a silent token between them that meant, "I love you." Four squeezes back from Hattie meant, "I love you, too."

Hattie lifted her head slowly and smiled weakly. Dakota's soft touch always made her feel better. Looking around the yard at the extensive crowd of people, Hattie decided she had been gone long enough. "Thank you everyone for bein' so supportive, but I think it would be best if I got back now. Talking to Dakota, she said, "I'll meet you and James in my study after the reception." James took Dakota's hand, and together, they walked back to the reception. Turning to Ira, Hattie smiled and said quietly, "Somehow, I've got to talk to you alone."

Shaking his head, Ira replied, "I'm sorry Hattie, my work with my uncle in Kansas City isn't finished yet, and I've got to be back on a train early tomorrow mornin'. I really wish I could stay, but I can't."

Her heart breaking at the thought of Ira leaving again so soon, Hattie whispered, "Ira, I promise that thin's will work out. You must have faith."

Ira, not knowing how things could ever work out, forced a smile, and after giving her one final embrace, he left the reception.

Quickly, Hattie returned to Abner's side and almost immediately was encouraged to sing again by Rebecca. Hattie gracefully accepted, and as Robert handed her a guitar, she announced, to everyone's delight, that she was going to sing with Lewis Beaumont. Lewis was a longtime friend of the family, and since he had been home tending to his mother, he had visited Hattie at Silver Creek quite often. He was a brilliant lawyer, for that is why Rebecca sought his council along with James, but he also had a brilliant tenor voice and had often sang with Hattie and her family at church socials and the like. The two of them had spent the days he was at Silver Creek writing songs.

Hearing Hattie announce his name, Lewis left his mother's side and headed to the makeshift stage. Standing next to Hattie, he was extremely good-looking. He had beautiful light complected skin and golden blond hair. He stood only a slender five foot seven inches tall, but carried himself proudly in a very stylish white suit that Hattie had had made especially for the occasion. His sultry eyes, high cheekbones, soft jaw line, and perfectly formed mouth were a direct result of his French heritage, and at first glance, even though he was a gorgeous man, he had an uncommon amount of feminine features. Strangely, no hair grew on his arms, his hands were very slender, and he had very narrow hips. Despite these oddities, he was still regarded as very handsome.

Smiling at Lewis, Hattie addressed the crowd. "This is a song Lewis and I have recently written since he has been home. It is a ballad of two lovers." As she began strumming her guitar and singing as few women could, she again captivated her audience. Lewis added just the right touch, singing beautifully alongside her, and together they swayed back and forth with the rhythm of the guitar.

Minerva and each of her children had been blessed with fine voices, and her own father, Elijah, had taught them to sing in three part harmonies while they were very young. Hattie, the most talented one among them, not only sang beautifully but also had been writing songs with Lewis Beaumont since she was ten.

Rebecca, knowing how talented Hattie was, and being very

proud of her, had wanted to show off her talents to her out of town friends and guests. The result was exactly as she had hoped, as everyone was spellbound by her charisma and charm.

As the orchestra joined in behind Hattie's guitar, Lewis stood up, walked off the stage, and made his way to his mother, Pansy, embracing her lightly. He loved his mother very much, and he didn't like it when she was ill. She, Minerva, and Samantha Saxon, Ira's mother, had all been Rebecca's best friends. So when Rebecca found out she was ill, she immediately called for Lewis to come home.

As Hattie sang, "I Hear Your Sweet Voice Calling Me," Lewis continued to move through the crowd, singing as beautiful as any Irish tenor and in perfect harmony with Hattie. Joining her back on the stage, he took her hand and they sang with all the tenderness they could find in their hearts. As Hattie's family joined in for the final chorus, the crowd was hypnotized. The song ended and for a moment not a sound could be heard, followed by another round of thunderous applause that began with Rebecca herself.

Then, as everyone became quiet again, Hattie played the moment for all it was worth. She announced that the song they had just heard was dedicated to her beloved Abner.

Abner stood, thanked everyone for their attendance and introduced the Governor and his party. The Governor's concluding remarks were that the citizens of Davies County could look forward to Abner Garland's candidacy for the State House of Representatives soon. That sparked a final round of applause, and the reception ended. Hattie went to Abner's side and suggested, for appearance sake, they stand where they could say goodbye to everyone and thank them one final time for attending the wedding. He readily agreed and his parents and Minerva joined them.

When everyone who was not a weekend guest had left, Hattie, Minerva, and Rebecca crossed the veranda to talk to Lewis and his mother Pansy.

Hattie greeted Pansy. "I'm so glad that you were able to come, Mrs. Beaumont."

"As of late, I've been a bit poorly, Miss Hattie. Time, I'm afraid, has caught up with me, as my body just doesn't work like it used too. Even the simplest of tasks wear me out these days, but in spite everything, I wouldn't have missed this for the world. Your wedding was just beautiful and to hear you and my Lewis singing was worth every bit of effort it took for me to come today."

Pansy Alexander was a small woman, well mannered, graceful, and from an aristocratic family in Georgia. Pansy's family's wealth was not quite as much Rebecca Garland, but it was very sizeable to say the least. They had been friends for years and their friendship was what had drawn Pansy to Davies County. She had married Robert Beaumont late in life, but was left a widow shortly after, as Robert was killed in a freak accident while breaking a horse. Lewis, tragically, was only a year old and never knew his father. Pansy had raised Lewis alone on her large farm, but at her late brother's insistence, when Lewis turned fifteen, he was sent to a Boston boarding school. Later he entered a New York City Law school and became an attorney. At twenty-five, Lewis was not only well educated, but also a very well-traveled man.

Hattie had sensed a strange uneasiness surrounding Lewis since he had arrived home recently. Something was definitely wrong and troubling him greatly. After a short visit with Pansy, she asked, "Come, Lewis, walk with me in the gardens."

Cautiously Lewis questioned, "Won't Abner be perturbed?"

"Go with Miss Hattie, Lewis, I'll attend to Abner," Rebecca insisted.

With Rebecca's approval, Lewis agreed. Hattie's friendship meant a lot to him, and today, more than ever, he needed to confide in someone. Because of Hattie's maturity and understanding nature, he felt he could talk to her easier than to anyone else in the world. In wisdom, Lewis considered her far wiser than her fifteen years.

As they reached the far edge of the gardens near the gazebo, Lewis took her hands in his. "Hattie," he began cautiously, making sure they were out of earshot of anyone else, "I need your help."

Hattie, sensing this was going to be something serious, led him to a nearby bench. Sitting down, she patted the place next to her, inviting him to sit beside her. "Of course, Lewis, whatever you need, I'm here for you."

Glad to hear he had her support, he let out a sigh of relief and continued. "Actually, I'm going to need a lot of help. I need to speak to Laville as well, and in time, the rest of the family."

Looking into Lewis's face as he talked, Hattie thought to herself, "My goodness, he sure is handsome, almost too handsome." His teeth were a brilliant white and his light blue eyes were surrounded by thick, blond eyelashes. Again she thought, "He has the kind of eyes most girls would die for." His golden blond hair was thick and wavy, but his features weren't rugged like Ira's or Abner's. She thought, "What girl in this county wouldn't give her eye teeth to catch a man like Lewis." Even Laville had mentioned several times how wonderful she thought he was, but he was too much like one of her own brothers for her to ever be interested. Realizing she had been lost in thought, she quickly reassured him that he would have the full support of the family no matter what he did. Then, becoming anxious, she entreated, "Please, Lewis, tell me what is bothering you."

Taking a deep breath and gathering all the courage he could muster, Lewis began to pour out his heart and soul to Hattie about his cousin. He explained exactly what had been tearing at the very fiber of his being for so long. He was brought nearly to tears when he admitted that he couldn't go on if he didn't acknowledge his feelings. "Things have to change for her and my mother," he explained to Hattie. "My hope is that you will support me every step of the way. I have placed my trust in you by telling you this. Please, Hattie, don't fail me."

Hattie sat in silence, as she ran what she had just heard over and over in her mind. She tried as hard as she could to figure out exactly what she could do to help Lewis and his cousin Lou.

Lewis, wondering why Hattie wasn't saying anything for such a long time, interrupted her train of thought. "Perhaps I shouldn't have gone into this so vividly," he said softly. "But you do understand exactly what direction I mean to take concerning Lou?"

Realizing that her reaction would be life changing, not only for Lewis, his cousin Lou, but her entire family as well, Hattie chose her words carefully. "Yes, Lewis, I understood what you said and you can be assured with a situation such delicate as this you will not only have my support but the support of the entire family as well."

"Are you sure, Hattie?"

Nodding her head affirmatively, Hattie stated emphatically, "Yes, of course I am. I'll be damned if something this important ever came up and I did not do everything in my power to help someone especially when it concerns you or your family Lewis."

"You must think I'm insane. I just didn't know what exactly I could do to help her. You understand that you will need to help support both her and my mother emotionally through all of this." Lewis said, hanging his head slightly.

"No, Lewis, I don't think you're insane. I know that if our places were reversed and it was one of my family members you wouldn't think twice about doing all you could to help us."

Raising his head up, Lewis took a deep breath. "My decision wasn't made lightly, I assure you. It's something I've been thinking about seriously for a long time."

Glancing down at her wedding ring, she turned it around and around on her finger. As she contemplated what to say next, a thought came to her that she thought might help. "Lewis, look," she said to get his attention. Holding the gorgeous diamond ring on her finger up to his face so he could see it, she tried to get her point across. "My marryin' Abner is proof that we all do things that don't seem rational at the time. What I mean is that marryin' Abner was the last thing in the world I ever thought I'd do." As she stopped to think of what to say next, she looked into Lewis' eyes. The beauty of his blue eyes captivated her heart and seemed to speak directly to her soul. She knew at that moment that Lewis was absolutely serious, and knowing that for as sure as the sun would rise, she had to help him any way she could. So, accepting the fact that this is the path Lewis had chosen, she gave him a big smile and embraced him. With tears in her eyes, she whispered in his ear, "I'll not fail you, Lewis. You *can* count on me, no matter what it takes."

Hearing her loving words, Lewis let out a weary breath. "Thank you so much, Hattie, for understanding. I can't tell you how much this means to me." Scooting slightly away from her, he wiped the tears from her eyes and continued. "You do understand, Hattie, that once I've gone on they will need you more than anything."

"I understand that, and if you can pull it off your cousin will be in a much better situation. Unfortunately, unlike with you, people are going to know that I probably married Abner for Rebecca's money and the social position that it will afford. And you know what, Lewis, they'll be dead right. I have got to live with the fact that everyone knows. Once Rebecca told me what she wanted to do, it didn't take me long to realize that if I really wanted somethin' better in this life for my family, I'd better accept Rebecca's offer. As for Rebecca, I know she had good reason, even if it doesn't sound right to another livin' soul." As she put her hands on Lewis shoulders, she sighed deeply. "I guess we all do thin's that don't seem rational to other people, but upon closer inspection, those thin's are exactly what we need." Then, with a smile, she rose to her feet and pulled Lewis up as well. "Now, you said you needed Laville and the rest of the family to help you. Is that still how you feel?"

"Absolutely. Even though most people don't care for Laville, I've always admired her for her beauty and willfulness. With so much ahead to be done, I am going to need her help and support just as much as I need yours."

"Alright, it's settled. We can start tomorrow. Could you come back at about noon as this is goin' to require a lot of plannin' and work? Maybe I'll have some ideas by then."

"Yes, Hattie, I can, but I want you to understand that I've wrestled with this problem ever since I learned that about my condition. Knowing how this would end, I had to find a way to help not only her but mother as well. I honestly don't know what else to do."

"Have you ever confided in your Mother about what you plan?"

"I've tried. But just like the rest of my family she thinks it's completely hopeless."

"Does anyone else know about this?"

"Not a soul."

"Shannon is your best friend. Why haven't you turned to him?"

"Oh, Hattie, I could never talk to him about this. I only told you because I felt you of all people would understand." Looking down into his hands, he continued, "I want you to know that I understand what I plan to do is not going to be easy."

Curious, Hattie questioned, "Doesn't the whole idea scare you?"

"Of course it does. It scares me to death. All I know is this is something I have to do. Believe me, if I had known about this long ago I would have made many different choices. I know come 'Hell or High Water' I have to get her and mother back together. What do you think Laville will say when I talk to her?"

"She's goin' to be shocked and bewildered, but she loves you just as I do."

"Could you find her? I need to talk with her today while I still have the nerve to talk about this as openly as I have with you."

"Absolutely." Kissing him gently, she took his hands in hers one final time. "I'll help you in any way I can, Lewis, I promise. Meet me here tomorrow at noon, and with Laville's help, we'll decide on a plan. I'm sure this will all work out, we've just got to have faith." As she left him alone in the gardens and went to the house to find Laville, she wondered about the far-reaching consequences that this change would have. One thing, though, was for sure. This would be an undertaking of giant proportions, and she prayed that Heavenly Father would guide her and her dear friend in the right direction.

Watching Hattie as she walked away, with her wedding dress and veil flowing in the breeze, Lewis considered her a vision of loveliness. He had always considered her quite a woman, but most of all, he knew she was a devoted friend. Then, the more he thought of it, the guiltier he felt, "I hope I don't regret dragging her into this mess."

Making her way back to the veranda, Hattie found Laville and told her that Lewis needed to meet with her in the garden. As she walked away, Hattie grabbed her arm. "Please be understandin' Laville, he really needs our help." Laville, caring for Lewis deeply for reasons dating back to childhood, nodded and hastily made her way across the yard to the gardens. Hattie, seeing her mother and Rebecca, made her way to them. Getting their attention, she stated, "I have some unfinished business with James; please keep Abner occupied." Entering her well-adorned study, she found James and Dakota anxiously waiting for her.

Meeting her half way across the room, James said, "Miss Hattie, let's get this done and get back to the family. We certainly don't want to put Abner on guard to anything else."

"I know, James," Hattie replied solemnly. "The way he's acted and the thin's he has said to me has me concerned for my safety, but I didn't want to say anythin' in front of Mama or Rebecca because I know how they worry." Reaching the desk, Hattie looked over the papers James had set out for her. "Is Judge Stepp aware of this will that I'm signin'?"

"Yes, and I promise everything is in perfect order." Seeing the worry in her face, James was quick to agree with her. "You're right in being concerned about yourself, Hattie. Personally, I think the man is capable of doing anything."

"I feel better knowin' that Shannon and John are goin' to sleep outside my bedroom door tonight, and extra men will be ridin' the property lines the next few days. Rebecca kindly offered to share her room with me, but I need some time to be alone and gather my thoughts. These past two months have been almost too much for me to deal with." Looking at the will, she asked, "You're sure Cody is my only beneficiary?"

"Yes, Hattie. The will is written exactly as you asked."

Taking the writing quill and dipping it in the ink, she signed it. "If somethin' happens, promise me you'll get Dakota out of the State before my will is read."

"I promise, but the boys and I intend to see that nothing happens to you." Handing James the will, she embraced them both and left the room to return to her mother on the veranda.

Several hours went by, and it was late in the evening when the family was finally left alone, with all the weekend guests having gone to bed. Exhausted from the long day, the family retired to the parlor at Rebecca's request. Even Mary and George Walsh, Rebecca's most trusted hired hands were in attendance. Rebecca, seeing that everyone was seated, smiled widely before starting to talk. "I want to thank you all for your support today. Especially you, Mary and George, thank you very, very much. Because of all your hard work, everything was carried out to the 'Tee'. It was just as Minerva and I had hoped." She paused. "Now that the wedding is over, perhaps we can move on to living our new lives. For as of today, the Silver Creek Estate and mansion now belong to Miss Hattie. I will remain here a short time then return to Silver Springs, my father's plantation outside Richmond. Miss Hattie has asked me to invite you, James, to bring your children and come live here with us. I know that you have been living alone in your house in Gallatin since your first wife's untimely death, but with you and Dakota planning to be married at

Christmas, it would give her, and the rest of us, a chance to grow closer to you and the children."

He replied gratefully, "I'm sure the children would love it, Rebecca. It would be a wonderful opportunity both for them and for me. In other words, I humbly accept."

After the family rejoiced over James's decision, the room grew silent, and Rebecca turned to her son. "Abner, now that this charade is over, I want you and your father to leave the estate before I retire this evening."

"What are you talking about?" he questioned indignantly. "This is my wedding night, and you have nothing to say about this. Personally, I've had planned on being with Miss Hattie tonight. Seeing as I'm not getting anything else out of this damn wedding, I sure as hell intend to have my bride." Turning, he hungrily looked at Hattie. "Tonight she'll understand what it's like to be a real woman."

"Abner, watch your mouth. For God's sake, you're in mixed company. I'll not have you disrespect me or anyone else in this house. I was hoping not to have to quarrel about this, but unfortunately, you are forcing me to take action. So, you listen to me, and listen well. There will be no consummation of this marriage. Not tonight or any other night. You are married to Miss Hattie in name only. She didn't marry you to put up with you or to bear your children. She married you so that she could be my legal heir."

"Damn it, Mother! You have no right to interfere!" he yelled.

The whole family came to their feet in rebellion, but Rebecca raised her hands gesturing for them to stay calm. "Take it easy, folks," she said as she encouraged them to sit down again. "Please excuse my son for his ill-mannered behavior, believe me, he has been taught better." She walked across the room and stood before her son. "Abner, I've taken all I intend to take from you, and I can see that you've not learned your lesson yet."

Turning to Jess, she said, "For once in your life, Jess, take control of our son. I want both of you, as I said before, to leave this house tonight before I retire. If you don't, I'll revoke the money I have set aside for both of you, and I'll send one of the boys for the Sheriff. I'll have you both legally removed from the estate and thrown in jail, if I must." Getting right in her husband's face, she said curtly, "You know darn well, Jess, your life won't be worth a plugged nickel without my money. Now, grab whatever you brought and get out! I'm in no mood to listen to your whiny-bagging or Abner's."

Jess took Abner's arm and forced him out of the room into the hall. "Don't raise a stink now, Son. Every dog has his day, and we'll have ours. Let's get out of here. They can have this damn place as far as I'm concerned." With that, the two men exited the house, mounted their buggy, and left.

Rebecca waited to speak until she saw out the window that Jess and Abner were indeed gone. With the room silent once again, she asked James to lead them in prayer. Looking around the room, Hattie realized again how important her family was in her life.

James poured out his heart in prayer, and a special spirit of peace fell over the Silver Creek Estate. This special spirit would be sorely needed to carry the family over the trials that would hang over the mansion like a dark cloud for many years to come.

***

The following day at noon, Hattie was in the gardens with Rebecca, when she saw Lewis approaching the house on horseback looking like a knight in shining armor. As Lewis dismounted, he saw Mary and George Walsh tending the shrubbery alongside the house.

Mary Walsh was a pudgy little woman, standing only five foot one inch tall. With dark red hair and green eyes pleasantly accentuating her round face, she was Rebecca's confidant and secretary. She enjoyed overseeing the cooking and actually did much of it herself. She was a warm loving person, Irish by nationality, and quite outspoken. It was also quite well known that she had absolutely no use for Abner or Jess and made no bones about it.

As for her husband George, he was director of the estate and did all the hiring. For many years he had served as Rebecca's right hand man. He, too, was of Irish descent, standing five feet seven inches tall and was built rather stocky. He was fair complected, blue eyed, and redheaded. He was intelligent and seldom let his temper get the best of him. Now in their late fifties, he and Mary had raised five children on the estate in a home Rebecca had built for them. Since the children were all grown and gone five years ago, Rebecca insisted that Mary and George live in the mansion with her.

Stopping when he reached the elderly couple, Lewis dismounted his horse and coughed to get their attention, as they were engrossed in their work. "Mrs. Walsh," Lewis asked politely, "I'm looking for Miss Hattie."

Mary greeted him with a big smile, having loved him since he was a child. Wiping the dirt from her hands, she reached out and gave him a big hug. "Sure enjoyed your singing yesterday, Mr. Lewis. Your singin' be as pretty as a nightingale. The sound of your voice made me think of me home back in Ireland." Her smile showed she meant what she said. "Miss Hattie be a walkin' in the side gardens with Miss Rebecca." She pointed across the yard to two figures beneath a large tree. "There they be right there."

Seeing Lewis coming toward them, Hattie and Rebecca walked to meet him. After greeting him, Rebecca excused herself and left them alone at the gazebo, their favorite spot at the estate.

Watching Rebecca walk away, he said, "She sure is a gracious lady, Hattie, you can learn a lot of important things from her."

Suddenly, the solution to Lewis's problem came to Hattie like a bolt of lightning out of the clear blue sky. "You're right Lewis," she said excitedly, "and so can you're cousin. I know exactly what we can do. Once you make all the preparations to transfer your estate to her and she and your mother arrive here they can stay here on the estate while you work through this whole thin'. We all care about you, and I think the boys will accept this if it is presented to them right."

"I don't know, Hattie, it's going to be quite a shock for your brothers. I've been thinking, and I'm not sure I want to chance it."

"Well, you'll never know until you talk to them, now will you?" Taking his hands in hers, she looked directly into Lewis's pretty blue eyes. "Whatever you decide, I'll support you and protect you and Lou with the last breath that's in me. I promise you that."

Once again tears filled his eyes, a lump formed in his throat and he could hardly speak. "I know you will, Hattie. I've been counting on it."

Returning to the house, Lewis mounted his horse and left with many thoughts running through his mind. He knew he needed Hattie and Laville, and Silver Creek would be the perfect place to fulfill his plan. But, as for her brothers, he doubted they would understand. Dare he take a chance and tell them his plans? He had to hold on, knowing that often, holding on was the hardest thing that life asks of us. Patience, prayer, and courage alone were not going to be enough, not for a task as monumental as he had in mind.

Chapter 6
FOOL THAT I AM

ONE WEEK FOLLOWING HATTIE and Lucinda Brown's conversation at Hattie's wedding, Lucinda rode down the long road to the estate and was met at the steps of the great mansion by George Walsh. As she stepped down from her father's buggy, she told George that she had only two bags. Knowing Miss Hattie was expecting Lucinda, he took her to Rebecca's study. "Miss Hattie is out for a walk with Rebecca. She asked if you would wait here in her study. I hope you don't mind."

Happy to even be invited into such a beautiful home, she replied graciously, "Not at all." It was some time before Hattie returned, giving Lucinda time to collect her thoughts. Sitting in a chair looking out the window, she fiddled with her dress. She was nearly sick, not knowing how she was going to tell Abner's mother of her situation. She hoped so much that Rebecca would accept her, and even though Hattie had said she would, Lucinda had reservations. Illegitimacy was not looked upon kindly, and she worried about her child growing up without a father. The more she thought about it, the more upset she got until, after a couple minutes, she was weeping uncontrollably in her hands. Just then, the ornate double doors to the study opened as Hattie and Rebecca entered the room. Standing and turning to face them, Lucinda's tear stained face showed the wear of much stress.

Rebecca, seeing Lucinda's hot tears, rushed to her side. "Lucinda, my dear, whatever is wrong? Come, come, Dear, sit down here on the settee and tell me what's troubling you."

As Lucinda joined Rebecca on the sofa, Hattie knelt on the floor beside them. Lucinda's mother Katherine was one of Rebecca's dearest friends, and Rebecca was with her when Lucinda was born. Lucinda had been a pretty child and grown into quite a beautiful woman, whom Rebecca loved very much. But now, sitting with Rebecca, a woman she had always looked up to, Lucinda was afraid and ashamed to have to tell her that her son had raped her. Finding it difficult to speak, Lucinda pleadingly looked to Hattie for help.

Rebecca was gifted in being emotionally in tune with those dear to her. Seeing the look in Lucinda's eyes, she patiently waited for her to speak. Finally, she asked Hattie, "Do you know what's wrong, dear?"

Hattie nodded, realizing this was going to break Rebecca's heart.

Seeing the expression on Hattie's face, Rebecca could sense that whatever was wrong had something to do with her son. "Please don't tell me, Hattie," she paused, "that this has something to do with Abner?"

Looking at Lucinda once more and then at Rebecca, Hattie replied hesitantly, "Yes, Rebecca, I'm afraid, it does." Taking her new mother-in-law's hands lovingly, she began to explain. "I found out only a short time before the weddin' that Abner had raped Lucinda, and now, she's goin' to have his baby." Rebecca didn't move as Hattie continued. "Do you remember questionin' me about the paper you saw on the vanity the day of the weddin'? It was to acknowledge the child as bein' Abner's and provide financial support for Lucinda until the baby is grown. I forced him to sign it, and he was so enraged that I became afraid for Lucinda. I've asked her to come to Silver Creek, so that we could help and protect her."

Rebecca began trembling but tried to remain calm. Inside she was raging at her son's deplorable behavior, but she knew she had to keep her emotions under control, as any lady of her upbringing must. Seeing the frightened look on Lucinda's face, she reached over and pulled her close and kissed her. "Hattie has done the right thing, Lucinda."

"Does that mean I can stay?"

"Surely you may; I wouldn't have it any other way. I'll cancel my trip to Richmond right away. I want you right here, and I promise you as I did Hattie, you'll never want for anything as long as you live." Tears ran down her face as she spoke, and taking a handkerchief from her sleeve, she blotted them. Hattie moved closer and rested one arm across Rebecca's lap. Rebecca was quiet for a long time, thinking of how much love she felt for these two beautiful young women. "How in the world could Abner have hurt them?" she thought. Her mind raced and her thoughts became more intense. Her great expectations for Abner were now utterly dashed to pieces by his base instincts and arrogant will. Standing, she walked to the door and called for George. "Lucinda will not be visiting, but will be living with us, George. I'll be discussing the matter with you, Mary, and the rest of the family later this evening."

Turning back to Lucinda, Rebecca said, "I don't want you more than a heartbeat away from me, and as God is my witness, I promise you that I will make up to you for everything that Abner has done."

As Lucinda left the study and followed George to her new room, Hattie stood and looked out the window at the blue Missouri sky. A moment later, she felt Rebecca standing next to her and felt her arm encircle her waist. "Tell me, Miss Hattie, are there any more surprises?"

"No, Ma'am, not that I know of. That was pretty much it. I am concerned, though, about Lucinda's parents, as they don't know yet. They have to know, of course, but Lucinda hasn't had the courage to tell them. I thought perhaps you and I could go there this comin' week and speak to them together."

"Yes, I agree, Lucinda has been through enough."

"I also thought perhaps I should share what you have given me with Lucinda, as there is so much."

"No, Dear, that won't be necessary. I'll take care of Lucinda. I still have a great deal of money, companies, and property in the South, along with my parent's plantation in Richmond." Rebecca's cheeks were still wet from tears. "I have maintained my father's fortune and invested wisely, Miss Hattie. It will be difficult in the beginning for you to comprehend the value of the immense holdings that I transferred to you yesterday."

Nodding sheepishly, Hattie said nothing, turned, and gazed at a portrait of Rebecca as a young woman, hanging above the mantle of a fireplace that was at the other end of the large, elegant study. The portrait was very beautifully done, as Rebecca was standing in front of Silver Springs, her parent's plantation. It depicted a young woman with long flowing blond hair and wind whipping about her dress. Gazing at it in admiration, Hattie thought to herself, "It's exquisite."

"I want you to know, Miss Hattie," Rebecca said quietly, "that I received a confirmation from the spirit of the Lord when I decided to give my fortune that day on your Uncle Paul's front porch. Never before have I received such a strong witness that what I was about to do was right." She paused, looked heavenward, and continued. "God has a mighty plan for you and I hope I live long enough to see just what it is."

Hattie sighed, as she considered what Rebecca was saying. Then, sensing Rebecca's sincerity, she responded with determination in her voice. "Whatever it is, I know Heavenly Father will make sure I'm up to meetin' it head on. For as it said, 'Nothin' is expected of the children of men, save the Lord shall prepare a way for us to accomplish it.'"

***

Three weeks later following supper one evening, George informed Rebecca that Jess and Abner were there but had not yet dismounted. Walking to the large front porch, she leaned against one of its six two-story ornately decorated pillars.

"Evenin', Rebecca," Jess said, almost too politely. "Abner and I thought we would drop by, sit, and visit a spell."

Rebecca, who was already aggravated because of their constant notes requesting more money, was having a hard time being civil. She was a smart woman, and despite the pretty smiles and polite gestures, Rebecca knew her kin's only motivation on this visit was money. Standing with her arms folded and tapping her foot, her temper flared, as she could no longer hold her tongue. "The hell you will... I'm sorry, Jess, but you're not needed nor wanted here. And if it's more money you're seeking, you're barking up the wrong tree. If I had any sense, I would have listened to my father's advice years ago and never married you. But 'fool that I am', I let my heart rule and it's been the biggest mistake of my life. Now, turn your horses around and get off this estate and out of my life!" Turning, she started for the door but stopped as Abner called to her.

"What about me, Mother? Don't you love me?" he asked, trying to play on her maternal heartstrings.

Turning around very slowly, she faced the two of them again. "Abner, you have turned out to be my greatest disappointment. I had once hoped you would become a great man, but coming from your father's loins, I'm afraid you have the moral integrity of a snake. You may be my flesh and blood, but that's where it ends. I don't see one thing in you that even remotely reminds me of my family. I will not have anything else to do with you, until such a time that I see some real changes made in your lifestyle and behavior. You must not only reform, but you must also repent for the heinous crimes you've committed. Until then, I don't want to look upon your face. You've hurt and embarrassed me for the last time. Your actions, where both Miss Hattie and Lucinda Brown are concerned, make me sick to my stomach. Mark my words, Abner. Lucinda is leaving here with me when I return to Richmond, and if you so much as touch her or that baby . . . ever . . . I'll cut you off without a penny and turn your sorry ass over to the law. Now, if you've got any sense at all, you'll leave with your Father and not return. Do I make myself perfectly clear?"

Knowing that nothing he could say would make any difference, he nodded affirmatively and replied bitterly, "Yes, Ma'am, perfectly. But you'll regret this."

"I'll what?" Her southern blood began to boil. "Why, you

indignant hellion! You turn that horse around and get out of here before I have George load a shotgun and have him fill that fancy bottom of yours full of buckshot."

Without another word, she turned, walked back into the house, and slammed the French doors behind her. Upon entering the grand foyer, she was startled to see James, Shannon, Robert, John, Hattie, and George Walsh all standing with guns drawn. Laughing, she said, "My, my, my, it does an old lady's heart good to know she can spout off like that and find an army like this behind her." Her laughter became contagious, and they all laughed with her.

Jess and Abner, hearing the laughter inside, were furious. They turned their horses around and rode away, not looking back. Rebecca, making her way to a window, watched them leave and hoped she'd seen the last of them.

Unfortunately, Abner wasn't that easily scared away, and the following night, under the cover of darkness, he slipped back into the mansion. Rebecca had been posting farm hands around the property at night since the wedding, but Abner was much too familiar with the estate and easily slipped past them. Still enraged at his Mother's treatment toward him, he intended to get back at her and Miss Hattie as well. Abner hated being played for the fool, and together, his mother and Miss Hattie had taken away everything that was important in his life. He had scores to settle, and he was only getting started.

Reaching the house, he entered quietly through a back door and made his way upstairs and down the hall to Hattie's bedroom undetected. Smiling slyly to himself that he had made it so easily, he slipped in. As he entered the room, he saw Hattie sitting at her desk in her nightshirt. Since her sister Dakota often slipped into her room in the evenings to visit, Hattie assumed it was her. Hattie folded the letter she had been working on and turned to speak, but before she could say anything, Abner grabbed her from her chair and struck her with his fist. The violent blow caused her to spin around, and as she fell blindly to the ground, her head struck the corner of her desk rendering her unconscious.

Leaning over her limp body, he ran his rugged hands wantonly over her. "I told you, Miss Hattie, that you'd regret crossing my father and me, but you wouldn't listen. Now, look at you, unconscious and blood running down your cheek. You think you're so smart, playing me for all I'm worth, then just casting me aside like a piece of trash. Well, I guarantee you that after tonight, you won't be able to forget me so easily."

Knowing he didn't have much time, Abner quickly picked up her body and placed it on the beautiful canopy bed. Lustfully, he looked down at Hattie in her nightshirt. He had dreamed of this moment for years. Only a simple piece of silk stood between him and the fruit that he coveted so. Finally, he couldn't take it anymore, and he ripped the nightshirt from her body. Pulling down his pants down, he violently thrust himself into her, and for the next few minutes, Abner had his way with Hattie exactly the way he had intended to all along. He moved in and out of her like a prowess lion, not being satisfied until he had at last emptied himself inside her. When he was finished, he pulled up his pants and punched Hattie several times so that she would remember exactly what was in store for her should she cross him again. Then, with the same stealthfulness that he had entered the house with, he walked quietly down the stairs and out the back door. He was gone before anyone was even aware that he had been there.

Not long after Abner had made his escape, Rebecca met Dakota in the hallway as Dakota made her way to Hattie's room. "Is that you, Rebecca?" Dakota asked.

"Yes, Dear, I was just on my way to see Miss Hattie. I wanted to say 'goodnight'."

"Me, too."

Reaching Hattie's door, Dakota had a very strange feeling. Rebecca knocked, and not getting an answer, knocked again. Again, there was no answer. "Let's go in, Rebecca," Dakota said with urgency. "Somethin's wrong, I can feel it."

Rebecca felt a chill run up her spine, as she turned the knob and pushed the door open. She started to call to Hattie when her eyes fell upon the ghastly scene. Hattie lay naked across the bed, and her torn nightgown lay on the floor. Rushing to her side, she saw large bruises across her face, and the blood that had trickled from her mouth was now dried on her face. "Oh my God," she cried out to Dakota. "She's been, she's been . . ."

"She's been what?" Dakota asked, sensing the fear in Rebecca's voice.

"Someone's attacked her. Please, Cody, find your Mama, quickly!" Rebecca placed a cover over Hattie, as Dakota made her way down the hall, calling out to her mother. Within minutes, all of the adults in the house were in Hattie's room, fear gripping their hearts. In desperation, Minerva sent John for old Doc Cowley, Gallatin's only doctor, as Hattie wasn't regaining consciousness.

Doctor Cowley arrived within the hour to find Lucinda sitting behind Hattie on the bed, holding her in her arms. After examining Hattie thoroughly, the doctor said she had suffered a concussion and, much to the family's dismay, had been brutally raped.

It was late the next morning before Hattie regained consciousness. At first, she was disoriented and couldn't understand what was going on. Then all at once, she remembered seeing Abner from the corner of her eye, and cried out. Rebecca took her hand and asked quietly, "Who did this?"

Hattie, still dazed, felt as though someone had punched her in the stomach, and her pelvis and legs seemed paralyzed. Looking straight into Rebecca's eyes, she hated to answer. Finally, she whispered, "It was Abner."

Immediately, Rebecca was overcome with grief, and Hattie's brothers were enraged. Together with James, they left to find him, but despite their best efforts, they could not find hide nor hair of Abner Garland. It was obvious he had skipped town, knowing they would be looking for him. The sheriff was notified, but with no one knowing Abner's location, there was little he could do. Abner had succeeded in getting even with Hattie, and though the family tried to console her with hopes that the worst was behind them, she knew in her heart that things were just getting started.

***

By early October, after nearly six weeks of rest, Hattie was fully recovered from the bumps and bruises sustained by the brutal attack. It was a bittersweet recovery for Hattie in the fact that even though she felt better, her recovery had required her to miss out on celebrating her sixteenth birthday on the twelfth of September. Hattie had wanted to have a gala party, inviting not only Ira back from Kansas City but also her many friends from Gallatin. Unfortunately, with Hattie's condition coupled with obvious security issues, it was just not possible.

Hearing about Hattie's horrible ordeal by telegram, Ira had wanted to come home, but at Hattie's insistence, Andrew Saxon convinced his son to stay in Kansas City as planned. Hattie felt embarrassed by the constant attention she was receiving during her recovery and said, "I don't want everyone to drop everythin' they're doin' just for me. I'm a strong girl. I'll be fine."

Hattie soon found out, though, that fine is a relative term. She had begun to notice that she was sick every morning and asked Rebecca to take her into town to see Doc Cowley. Her greatest fear became a reality, when the doctor told her that she was pregnant. Rebecca was absolutely beside herself because she had promised to protect Hattie and had failed terribly.

Both lost in their thoughts and hardly speaking, the ride back to the house seemed twice as long. Rebecca was numb, and the movement of the wagon back and forth made Hattie nauseous. Never, not even in her wildest dreams, had Hattie thought that her first child would be conceived through the horror of such an act. "Thank God," she thought, "that I was unconscious. I don't think I could have dealt with it otherwise, and I don't know how Lucinda has been able to."

Rebecca placed her arm around Hattie. "My dear, dear, Hattie, what have I done?"

"You," Hattie stated emphatically, "haven't done anythin' wrong. This isn't your fault. If it's anyone's fault, it's mine. I married Abner with the intention of havin' absolutely nothin' to do with him. 'Fool that I am', I mocked God."

"But I promised to protect you. Can you ever forgive me?"

Hattie pulled the horse to a stop, wanting to get something clear with Rebecca before they got home. "Abner had left the house.

None of us could have anticipated his comin' back. You did everythin' you could to protect me with the hired hands walkin' the property and all. What happened was not your fault, and I won't have you punishin' yourself over it. Nothin' can change the fact that I'm havin' Abner's baby. Regardless of how it was conceived, this is my baby, and your grandchild, and I will love it, just as Lucinda will love hers."

After they returned home, they called the family together and explained Hattie's condition. James and Hattie's brothers were so furious that their anger could not be soothed.

Rebecca rose from her chair, and the room fell silent. "I've had Sheriff Sanders notify the sheriffs of the surrounding counties to be on the lookout for Abner. I cut off all his assets and his yearly deposits the day after the attack, and I have now decided to place them in your name, Lucinda. Lastly, I filed the divorce papers, so that Hattie can legally be rid of Abner. I had thought we would wait an entire year before going ahead with the divorce, but obviously, Abner's actions have forced us to expedite matters." No one said a word as she continued. Her mother's heart was wrenching, but she had taken all she could from her son. "Abner must be brought to justice. His actions have clearly ended his political career or any other decent undertaking he may have ever wanted, and I swear to you all, even if he is my son, I'll not rest until he is behind bars." She looked around the room with tears forming in her eyes. "All of you are my family now, and you are the only thing that matters to me."

James and Hattie's brothers kept insisting that they be allowed to organize a wide scale search for Abner and take care of the matter themselves.

Hattie knew she must set the tone if those in the family were going to accept this as anything other than a tragedy. "I know that you all love me, but I'll not let Abner, nor what he has done, cause us to take the law into our own hands. We certainly can't go out and shoot him. He is Rebecca's only child, and we certainly can't put her through another heartache. You all know that I've always wanted to have children, and regardless of the fact that this baby's father is Abner, Rebecca is the grandmother and this baby will be a Morran. What child could possibly want for more than that? We must remember that God is in control of our lives. He always has been and always will be. Let's try to be up to what He has in store for us. I, for one, have forgiven Abner, and the rest of you must do the same. We're a strong family and no one can take our dignity away from us."

James, sitting near the window, stood and took the floor. "Miss Hattie, no one could have a better attitude about what has happened than you. I have always admired you for your spirit, your honesty, and most of all your faith but never so much as I do right at this moment. I want you to know that when I marry Cody, it will be an honor to become a member of this family, and whatever happens, I cast my lot with you."

Minerva, very taken with James's soft spoken words, made her way across the room and kissed his cheek. "I think we've been lackin' somethin' very important in this special family of ours." She paused and looked lovingly at James. "We need a patriarch. Don't you think, Rebecca?"

All eyes turned to Rebecca, and she agreed, knowing exactly what Minerva was suggesting. "Yes, Minerva, we do. And after all that we have witnessed here this evening, on top of his outstanding leadership over the past months, I think we've found our leader in

James. I, for one, can't think of a better man for the job." James bowed his head in humility, as Rebecca walked over to him and placed her hands on his strong shoulders. "Those of you who are willing to support and sustain James as patriarch of this family, please stand to your feet." Everyone stood as a witness of their support.

"I don't know quite what to say," he said, looking around the room into their faces. "I promise you that I will do my best to be worthy of your trust and support." Quietly everyone knelt in a circle, and James somberly led the family in prayer. With James's reverent words setting the tone, each of them agreed that they would fight against evil the best that they could, every day, for the rest of their lives.

Chapter 7
IT TAKES FAITH

CHRISTMAS 1896 ARRIVED QUICKLY and was accompanied by the long anticipated wedding of James and Dakota. Although Dakota had no preference in the matter, James had specifically wanted to have the wedding on Christmas Day. Being a very spiritual man and loving the winter for its simple beauty, he felt a special calmness and peace in the winter months that as he said, "Just isn't there during the rest of the year." So, with the elegant Silver Creek Estate decorated in the most beautiful winter trimmings and Rebecca again going overboard with the guest list, Missouri society's second biggest wedding of the year got under way.

Dakota, a dainty figure with auburn hair and blue eyes, looked absolutely stunning in her long flowing wedding gown and was complimented perfectly by her sisters and Lucinda, who were all wearing brilliant emerald green bridesmaid dresses.

Rebecca, knowing the weather would be less than comfortable, had a special tent set up that attached to the veranda and cascaded perfectly out over the court area, stopping just shy of the gardens almost fifty yards away. To keep the large number of guests warm during the ceremony, Rebecca lined the tent with special wood burning stoves and had her hired hands feeding them constantly. It was a giant undertaking, but as she and Minerva had done with Hattie's wedding before, they took on a monumental task and made it look easy.

Things got underway just after eleven in the morning with Shannon walking his sister down the red carpeted aisle to the wooden altar at the far side of the tent. Lovingly, he gave her away to James, who was waiting eagerly. Newton, it seemed, was nowhere to be found, which sat just fine with the rest of the family. Dakota, Hattie thought, had said it perfectly, "I don't care if we ever hear from him again. After everything he has done to this family, he is the last person I want to give me away. Mama was right. Pa's only use for us daughters was to gain the things he wanted."

As the wedding neared its conclusion, Rebecca turned and signaled to George to take his place at the front of the tent. Rebecca, it turned out, had a special surprise for everyone in the audience, but to make it work, she needed George's help. As George took his position, Rebecca waited anxiously for the moment to arrive.

The Reverend, knowing what Rebecca and George were planning, continued with the final vows. Then, as the moment arrived, he glanced at George before voicing with great pride, "I now pronounce you man and wife!" At the exact same moment the Reverend glanced at him, George began pulling on a rope in the corner. As he pulled, the crowd took in a collective breath as the far end of the tent rose up like the curtain on a Broadway stage, exposing the most breathtakingly gorgeous winter scene that any of them had ever seen. With snow cascading down in big puffy flakes, it was if all of Silver Creek was a giant snow globe and God had shaken it for all the guests to see.

With an endless sea of white as their backdrop, the newly married couple delicately kissed, and the crowd erupted into thunderous applause. Rebecca shed a tear as the moment turned out exactly as she dreamed it would be, utterly beautiful.

Locking arms, James and Dakota turned to walk back down the aisle and back inside the mansion to the immense and elegantly decorated ballroom (also known as the grand parlor) where the reception was to be held.

Hattie, standing up front, continued to gaze out at the snow covered gardens. As her eyes hungrily consumed the beauty before her, she thought back in her mind about all that had happened in the past year, and in doing so, one thing became abundantly clear. "Despite Pa's antics and the trouble that Abner has caused me, this has been a great year, and today provided the perfect endin'. My only hope is that the years that follow will be as wonderful as this one has been."

Truly happy, Hattie turned and walked down the aisle to join the rest of the family in the mansion. Little did she know, however, that the future held more adversity and tragedy then she ever could have imagined. For in the tumultuous year ahead, the deep faith she held in God and the support of her family, more than ever before, would have to carry her through.

***

The first six weeks of 1897 went just as Hattie had hoped, very well. With lots of hustle and bustle about the mansion and having been a very lonely woman most of her life, Rebecca was delighted that so many people were now living with her. Jess had selfishly denied her the large family she had always wanted, by refusing to allow her to have any other children than Abner. Now the mansion was finally fulfilling the purpose of its construction on such a grand scale, as the sound of music and laughter rang throughout its rooms and halls.

Things quickly turned for the worse, though, as Abner resurfaced on a snowy Sunday in late February. With his funds nearly exhausted, Abner knew the easiest place to get money would be to steal it from his mother. Thinking the family would be in church, he rode his horse across the back of the estate and through the snow covered fields to the house. Surprised to hear Hattie and Lucinda's voices in the parlor and George and Mary's in the kitchen, he debated leaving, but remembering just how low on money he was, he decided it would be worth the risk. Quietly, Abner entered the house and made his way upstairs to his Mother's bedroom where he knew money was kept in her private safe.

It was unseasonably cold that morning with near blizzard conditions, but being very spiritual, it took more than a little snow and wind to keep the family from church services. Also, unbeknownst to the rest of the family, the day's service held additional importance, as this was the day Hattie had told Lewis to come out to Silver Creek to put his plan into motion. He was to tell his mother that he was leaving for Europe that day, and then, as soon as church was over, he would make his way to the mansion.

As the family readied themselves for the trip into Gallatin, Lucinda started to have pains that Rebecca attributed to the pregnancy, and thus she suggested that Lucinda stay home. Seeing how cold it was outside and not wanting Lucinda to have to stay alone, Hattie volunteered to stay with her good friend. Lucinda was now in the eighth month of her pregnancy, and Hattie was just into her sixth. As the girls sat in the parlor reading scriptures aloud to pass the time, George and Mary worked in the kitchen baking pies and preparing an early dinner.

Becoming chilly, Hattie decided to get a blanket from the upstairs linen closet. As she slowly made her way across the grand foyer to the stairs, Hattie noticed snowy footprints. Knowing they were too large to be George's, she wondered where they came from. Her curiosity was soon satisfied, however, as she finished climbing the long grand staircase to the second floor. Much to her dismay, she saw none other than Abner backing out of his mother's bedroom. Enraged and shocked, she gasped causing Abner to whirl around in her direction. Having his full attention, she said angrily, "What in the hell are you doin' here?" Angry that he had been found out, he answered indignantly, "None of your damn business!"

"Oh, but yes it is. This is my house now, and you have no right to be here." Looking down, she saw that he had a handful of cash. Shaking her head in disbelief, her blood began to boil. "You just won't quit, will you? Stealin' from your own mother."

"She's got plenty. She'll never miss this!"

Pointing to the stairs, Hattie had reached her breaking point. "Get out, Abner! Take the money, get out, and don't come back!"

"Don't get snippy with me, you little bitch. I'll get out of this house when I'm damn good and ready!" Realizing she was pregnant, he said sarcastically, "So, you went out and got yourself pregnant. Tell me, who does the little bastard belong to?"

Hattie's green eyes narrowed, and the look of hate in them could have killed. "The child is yours, Abner, but you'll never have any claim to it. I'll see to that!"

Abner was furious. His eyes were aflame with anger and his cheeks turned deep red, as he grabbed Hattie and dragged her to head of the staircase. Looking down at her, he slapped her violently across the face. "How dare you spout off to me like that?" Then, with an evil smile working its way on to his face, he laughed slightly. "You still don't get it do you? I am going to do exactly as I want whenever I want. And there is nothing you can do about it." With that, he picked her up and shamelessly slung her down the stairs.

Hattie screamed as she fell blindly, hitting stair after stair until she reached the bottom banging her head on the floor, rendering her unconscious.

Knowing he had little time, Abner hurried down the stairs. Stepping over Hattie's limp and bleeding body, he stopped abruptly. "Never see my child, huh? Well, I'll just take care of that." Without hesitation, he drew back and began to kick her directly in her womb.

Lucinda, thinking she heard Hattie yelling at someone, had walked to the kitchen to tell George and Mary. She reached the kitchen just as they heard Hattie's blood curdling scream. Running down the hallway, they entered the grand foyer just in time to see Abner kicking her unmercifully.

Horrified, Lucinda screamed at Abner. "My God, Abner, what are you doing? Stop it! You'll kill her!"

Stopping in mid kick, he snarled at her. "Mind your own business, tramp."

Mary was furious to see Abner had returned to the estate after everything that had already happened. Thinking quickly, she grabbed the revolver the family kept in the table drawer in the hallway. Pointing it straight at Abner, she yelled as loud as she could. "Back off, Abner! Back off I say, or I be a shootin' you where you be a standin'."

Knowing Mary as he did, Abner knew that she would do exactly as she threatened. She had never liked him and had told him so many times.

Worried that Mary wasn't thinking rationally, George took the gun from her. Walking toward Abner himself, he yelled, "I'll not let her shoot you, Abner. You're not worth the powder it be a takin' to blow you to hell and back, let alone for her to hang for. But as for me, I have no qualms about puttin' you to rest, so if you be havin' a brain in your head you'll be a getting' away from me girls before I blow your frickin' head off."

Visibly shaken, Abner slowly backed up to the front door, put his hand on the knob behind him, and bolted outside, but not before George put three bullets in the door.

Kneeling over Hattie, Mary cried out to her husband, "Glory be to God, George! Ye best be a goin' for Doc Cowley and quick! Looks like our little Miss Hattie be in mighty serious trouble."

Before Mary had even finished her sentence, George ran down the main hall and out the back door to the barn. Knowing the good Doctor would be in church, he took a buggy and headed for Gallatin on the slick snowy roads as fast as he could. With the main road full of deep, half frozen wagon tracks, it kept him from making good time. Fearing for Hattie's life, his heart was pounding as he reached the church. Inside, he found Doc Cowley and quietly told him Miss Hattie had been seriously injured. Then, making his way to the family, he told them the same. Lewis, seeing George and Doc Cowley scrambling out of the church, sensed something was terribly wrong. Turning to his mother, he decided to expedite his plans and follow them back to Silver Creed immediately. Taking her hands in his, he slowly and deliberately told her the story Hattie and he had talked about then kissed her gently on the cheek. Making his way to the back of the church, he turned one last time to her and mouthed the words, "I love you, Mother," before disappearing out the doors into the driving snow.

Seeing him leave, a wave of uneasiness came over Pansy Beaumont, and though see didn't know exactly what it meant, she was fairly certain that she had seen her son for the last time.

Within an hour of the initial attack, George arrived back at the estate with Doc Cowley, followed close behind by Lewis. Jumping from the buggy as it rolled to a stop, the doctor, slipping and sliding on the freshly fallen snow, made his way to the front porch and entered the mansion. Crossing the grand foyer to the bottom of the staircase, he knelt beside Hattie's bruised, lifeless body and surveyed the situation. She had a small pillow beneath her head and was covered to keep her warm.

"We be afraid to move her, Doc," Mary said in tears.

"Good. You did the right thing, Mary. Has she regained consciousness, yet?"

"No, Doc, she ain't moved a muscle."

Examining Hattie, he shook his head worriedly. "We've got our work cut out for us this time, Mary. She's going to give birth to this baby prematurely, and we'll be damn lucky if we don't lose her and the baby."

Lucinda, kneeling on the floor next to Hattie, brushed Hattie's blood stained hair away from her face. "She just can't die, Doctor," Lucinda said tearfully.

Doctor Cowley again shook his head. "I'm sorry, Lucinda, but I just don't know if she's going to make it."

Lewis's worst fears were confirmed as he entered the mansion and heard the Doc giving Lucinda the horrible news. Making his way to stairs, he knelt next to Lucinda and looked upon the ghastly scene. Hattie was so badly hurt that he could hardly control his emotions. He felt like crying, but he held back as he looked straight into the Doctor's eyes. "She's going to live, Doc."

"What makes you so sure, Lewis?"

"Because God won't let her die and neither will I. Not this way, not now."

Doctor John Cowley had brought both Hattie and Lewis into the world, and he knew how close they had always been. Patting Lewis's shoulder, he forced a smile. "I'm not a very religious man, Lewis, you know that. I mean, I go to church and everything, but I'm afraid it is going to take more than faith to save Hattie this time." Pausing, he looked around at everyone present. "This time it will take a miracle."

Fighting with his emotions, Lewis replied, "Just do all you can, Doc. If it takes a miracle, then that's what will happen."

Doc Cowley shook his head in amazement. "Well, with faith like that, Lewis, we can't lose. Come now, help me carry her upstairs." Turning to Mary, he started giving instructions. "We're going to need some hot water and towels, Mary. This isn't going to be pretty, but if we hurry, we might have a shot."

The next buggy arrived just as Lewis and Doc Cowley were starting up the stairs with Hattie. Minerva and Rebecca were the first to enter the house, and upon entering, George pulled Minerva aside. "Miss Minerva, you need be strong if Miss Hattie be survivin' this one. She be needin' all your strength, prayers, and love."

After parking the buggy in the barn, Shannon, Robert, and John ran through the snow and leaped up the stairs onto the porch. Robert, reaching the still open door, was terrified as he saw his sister limply hanging from Lewis's arms with her long red hair almost dragging the stairs. "My God," Robert screamed, "What's happened?"

"Hattie's been seriously injured," Doc Cowley replied as they reached the second floor landing.

Turning to George, Rebecca was beside herself. "Tell us exactly what happened."

"Abner, the dog, he came back. Threw poor Miss Hattie down the stairs, he did. Then, if that wasn't bein' bad enough, he kicked her wee body over and over again at the bottom of the stairs here."

"Oh, George, no!" Rebecca cried from the depths of her soul, before falling limply into Minerva's arms.

"I thought Mary be a shooting him, so I took the gun from her," he continued.

Hearing what George said, Robert turned to his brothers in anger. "If I find him, I'll kill him!"

"No!" Mary shouted, as she started up the stairs with the supplies the doctor had wanted. "That be exactly what Miss Hattie wouldn't want you to be a doin'."

Robert replied, "You're one to talk, Mary. Why, it sounded like you intended to shoot him?"

"Maybe she did," George confessed, "but the fact is, she didn't. You can't be a goin' off on some wild goose chase tryin' to find him. Best be lettin' his Mother take care of this. You boys be a stayin' right here as we be a needin' everybody."

Rebecca, still in Minerva's arms, shook her head in disbelief. "This just can't be happening," she told herself in her mind. "As if it wasn't bad enough that Abner raped Miss Hattie, now he tried to kill her and their unborn child." She was trying hard to keep her wits about her, but she was so angry that she could hardly think straight.

The last buggy arrived about fifteen minutes later with James, Dakota, Laville, and the four younger Morran brothers. They had gotten stuck in the ever deepening snow and had to dig themselves out. Entering the parlor, George explained the whole ordeal to those who just arrived. Knowing that Doc Cowley would need plenty of time to tend to Hattie and her unborn baby, the family settled in for a long wait.

The minutes seemed like hours, and the hours seemed like days, as the family anxiously waited for any word of what was happening. Shannon worriedly paced the floor as little Miles cried on John's shoulder. Patience was growing thin when finally they heard a door close followed by someone walking down the hallway. A moment later, Mary stood with her hand on the railing of the second floor balcony overlooking the grand foyer. Anxiously, the family rushed in to hear what she had to say. The look on her face caused them all to fear the worst. Slowly, she descended the stairs, and upon reaching the bottom step, she sat down, wiping away tears. Mary, unable to speak at first, took a minute to gain control of her emotions. Then, with the family gathered around her in a circle, she explained what happened. "Miss Hattie delivered her baby, and the wee one, a little girl she be, lived but only a moment."

As tears of anguish filled his eyes, Robert, unable to contain his anger any longer, started for the door. Rebecca, who had walked to the balcony as well, saw Robert about to leave and knew what he was thinking. Not wanting him to take matters into his own hands, she called to him. "Please, Robert, go for the Sheriff. Abner must be found and brought to justice." Robert nodded his head and left immediately.

Laville, who had been suffering from a headache all day, was about to ascend the stairs to ask Doc Cowley if he had any medicine to take away the pain, when she suddenly blacked out. Falling down, she hit her head slightly on the stair rail before John could swoop in behind her, catching her. The headaches were nothing new to the family, as Laville had been suffering from them since she was a child. They were quite excruciating and often left her unconscious.

John, knowing what to do, asked Lucinda to fetch him a wet washcloth. Upon her returning, he took the washcloth and dabbed Laville's head lightly. As he did, she slowly came to. Then suddenly, as if she just remembered something, she looked at John with deep concern. "Is Hattie going to be all right?"

John, taken aback by her sincerity, shook his head. "We're not sure, Laville. Not even Doc Cowley knows."

Shannon, also surprised at Laville's apparent concern for Hattie, watched in amazement as Laville quickly got up out of John's arms and rushed up the stairs toward Hattie's bedroom. "What in the world has come over her?" he asked James, who was standing next to him.

A bit surprised himself, James remarked, "I don't know, but it's said that sickness and death do strange things to people."

Reaching Hattie's bedroom door, Laville rushed in without knocking and found the doctor and her mother cleaning up the remains of Hattie's baby's birth. It was obvious by the rags that Hattie had hemorrhaged badly. Lewis stood looking out the window with tears streaming down his face. In his arms he held Hattie's tiny baby, lifeless and cold. Dakota Jayne, who had stayed next to Hattie all the while the Doc was working on her, stood heartsick with her arm about Lewis's waist.

Laville, still in the dress she had worn to church, hastened to Hattie's side and began helping her mother, and within minutes, she too was covered in blood. Grief stricken, Rebecca returned to the room and stood watching.

Doctor Cowley, watching Laville, was thankful to see her helping. As Hattie lay unconscious, she took a comb from her own hair and combed Hattie's bloody hair away from her face. The bruising from the fall down the stairs was now profound and Hattie's face was badly swollen. Finding it hard to speak, Laville turned to Doc Cowley concernedly. "Is she going to die?"

The Doctor shook his head, "I don't know, Laville. I honestly don't know."

"I love her, Doctor, please don't let her die!"

Minerva could hardly believe what she was hearing. This was not at all like Laville. Not once had she ever heard Laville say she loved Hattie. If anything, it had always been just the opposite.

Laville, tears streaming down her face, left Hattie and went to Lewis, placing her hand on his shoulder. If there was anyone for whom Laville truly cared about, it was Lewis. He had risked his own life and saved her from drowning when Laville and Hattie were children.

He turned and spoke in a whisper so that Rebecca couldn't hear. "This should never have happened, Laville. Even knowing Abner as I do, I can't believe he would do this. I swear I'll get even with that fiend even if it takes me the rest of my life."

Dakota asked tenderly, "May I hold the baby?" Taking the lifeless child in her arms, she turned to Laville and asked, "Who does she look like?"

Their mother, who had just joined them at the window,

answered instead. "She looks very much like you, Laville, at your birth. No doubt she would have been beautiful."

Laville smiled as Lewis put his arm around her. Noticing that Rebecca had taken a chair in the corner and was sitting with her face in her hands crying, Laville quietly implored to Lewis, "I think you ought to try to comfort Rebecca. She's taking this harder than anyone."

"I will," he said, as he kissed her cheek. Walking across the room, he knelt in front of Rebecca and said tenderly, "Come, Rebecca, let's go downstairs. You look exhausted, and besides, there's nothing else any of us can do here."

"Oh, Lewis, I just can't," she said in between sobs. "I'm so afraid Miss Hattie will die. All I ever wanted to do was to make life better for her, and it seems that all I've done, in one way or the other, is bring her pain."

"That's not true, Rebecca. All you've done is show her kindness and love. Every young woman should be so lucky to have a mother in law like you."

Smiling weakly, she appreciated his kind words. "Still, I have not done my part to properly protect her. I have been wracking my brain ever since the first time Abner attacked her, and I've come to the conclusion, now more than ever, that the only way she will truly be safe is if she has bodyguards with her at all times."

"Bodyguards," Lewis questioned?

"Yes, bodyguards. It is not uncommon for people of extreme wealth and power to have many bodyguards accompany them. I don't know exactly who I'll find or where I'll find them, but I am going to have James start looking immediately. One way or another, Hattie must be protected, or the poor thing won't live to see her seventeenth birthday."

Nodding his head, he knew she was right. "You realize, though, that it will take months to find the right men. Not to mention the time it will take to train them as a team. Needless to say, it won't be easy."

"I understand that, Lewis, but I'm afraid that there is nothing left for me to do. The Sheriff can only do so much, and given how cunning Abner is and how many crooked friends he and his father have in the surrounding counties, I doubt the authorities will ever find him. That leaves me with only one choice: to take matters into my own hands. And as God as my witness, I will find a way to guarantee Hattie's protection. I don't care how expensive it is. She means too much to me."

Taking her arm, Lewis helped her to stand and wiped the remaining tears off her face. Silently, they exited the room and walked to the grand staircase.

Laville, seeing them leave, quickly joined them, and as she took Rebecca's arm said, "She'll not die, Rebecca. We'll not let her. Hattie is too special for her life to end like this. Even I feel that God has a great plan in store for her, and he will not let her die before she does what He sent her to do. I think we need to remember what Hattie always says, 'we must have faith.'

"I'm a bit surprised, Laville; I've never heard you talk like this before."

"Just because I don't say something, doesn't mean that I don't think it," Laville replied quickly.

Minerva, who had left Hattie's bedroom before them and was now waiting at the head of the staircase, noticed a different look on Laville's face that she had never seen before. It was one of love, gentleness, and compassion.

Seeing Minerva standing there, Laville reached out and grabbed her hand. "I don't know what comes over me sometimes, Mama. I'm sorry for the trouble I've caused you. Please forgive me."

Minerva, flabbergasted, looked deep into Laville's eyes and was shocked at what she saw. It was as if she was looking into the eyes of a stranger, and instinctively, her mother's heart knew this wasn't an act. She was one hundred percent sincere. Overwhelmed, Minerva kissed her on the cheek, which was something Laville seldom permitted.

"Arrangements need to be made for the baby, Minerva," Lewis said quietly.

"Let me take care of that, Mama. If you don't mind?"

"That would be fine, Laville. You know what needs to be done."

Letting go of her mother's hand, Laville turned and took Lewis's arm. "I'd like for you to help me."

"Are you sure?"

She nodded her head, and together, they walked downstairs.

Rebecca stood bewildered. "What's coming over her, Minerva?"

Minerva, perplexed herself, replied, "I don't rightly know. She's always been a strange child, and seldom has she showed compassion toward anyone. If she did, it was just for a short time and then right back to her old indignant self."

As Laville and Lewis descended the stairs, the family was shocked to see Laville's dress stained with blood. "Oh, Miss Laville," Mary said sadly, "your dress, your beautiful dress, it be ruined."

Stopping and looking at her dress, she realized Mary was right, but to Mary's surprise, she didn't care. "It's only a dress," she sighed, "a dress can be replaced, Mary, a sister can't."

Touched by her compassion, Mary suggested sweetly, "Come, let's be gettin' you a dress from Miss Hattie's spare closet in her study."

Following Mary, Laville paused to speak to John, "Please, after I've changed, would you take the dress out back and burn it, along with the other things which are going to be brought downstairs." John nodded that he would but was shocked that Laville had actually said please. Turning to Shannon, she asked, "Could you please go into town and tell Mr. Scarborough, the undertaker, that our niece needs a coffin for a proper burial tomorrow. Also, please stop by Reverend Walker's. I think Mama and Rebecca would like for him to come out right away." Shannon and John looked at each other in amazement. This was not the sister they were used to.

"Please!" she entreated again, "This is no time to dawdle. There's so much to do for Hattie and the baby."

As the brothers left, Lewis heard Dakota descending the stairs behind them, and turning asked, "Cody, has Hattie come to yet?"

"Not yet, and Doc Cowley is getting' pretty worried."

Seeing Mary return with a new dress, Laville met her and went back into Hattie's study to change. Afterwards, as they returned to the main hallway, Mary suggested that they retreat to kitchen to eat something. "It's been a long day, lass, and it be hard for a body to think on an empty stomach. You best be gettin' off your feet for a spell, as I be thinkin' it be a long night as well."

James took Mary's arm as they entered the kitchen. Her accent seemed to get thicker the more tired she became, and James recognized it. "I think it's you, Mary, who ought to be taking a break. You look worn out."

"Oh, Lordy be, don't be a worryin' about me, Mr. James, I be a doin' fine. It's Miss Hattie I be a worryin' about. The Lass never harmed a soul in her life, and to be seein' her in this condition, I'm afraid, is just too much for me to be a handlin'."

The night proved to be just as Mary had predicted. The Sheriff arrived not long after Reverend Walker, and Rebecca, wanting justice, asked him to form a posse and find Abner. The Sheriff did so, charging Abner with actions that led to the death of his daughter and attempted murder of his wife.

Lewis refused to leave Hattie's bedside that night, and the next morning at a little after 11:00, he stood silent at her bedroom window. Outside in the cold and biting wind, the family was gathered around the gravesite of Hattie's baby daughter.

Reverend Walker stood in reverence at the head of the tiny coffin. Loving Rebecca and Minerva very much, he felt their pain. Turning to Minerva, he asked, "What's the child's name?"

Minerva hesitated, realizing for the first time the child was unnamed. Wiping a tear from her eye, she shook her head. "I don't know, Reverend, Hattie hasn't regained consciousness and…"

Laville, interrupting Minerva before she could finish, raised her voice so everyone could hear. "Faith, Reverend Walker, the child's name is Faith Garland."

Minerva stood stunned. "Why, Laville, you can't name Hattie's child!"

"And just why not? She can't name her, Mother, and the child is about to be buried for God's sake. Surely one of us standing here should be allowed to name her. I don't know about the rest of you, but I won't have Hattie's baby buried without a name. I repeat, Reverend Walker, the child's name is Faith."

"Why Faith, Laville?" Rebecca questioned curiously.

"Because Hattie's whole life is based on faith. After all, isn't it 'faith' that Hattie is always telling us we should have? When she comes to, she's going to need all the faith she can draw on, especially when she finds that her tiny daughter lived only a minute or two and was returned to heaven before she could even see her."

Dakota Jayne, seeing no harm in the name, came to her sister's defense. "Mama, I know I don't agree with Laville much, but I think she's right on this. It's goin' to take all the faith we have to pull Hattie through this."

Robert, the most tenderhearted of all the older boys, broke down and began to cry. Quietly, his mother asked, "Then we're all in agreement?" They all nodded their heads yes. "Very well, Reverend Walker, Faith Garland is the child's name."

Lewis, still watching from the second story window, clinched one hand in the other until his knuckles were white. Though he appeared to be handling this tragedy, the pain inside was almost more than he could bear. Looking down, he could see Reverend Walker giving his sermon, and once finished, Lewis saw James bow his head and lead the family in prayer. As everyone slowly parted and walked back to the house, Lewis turned and looked at Hattie, so still and pale. Memories of her youth flooded his mind like a raging river over a waterfall, with her 12th birthday standing out. He marveled how uncannily accurate she, at twelve, was with her Uncle Paul's six shooter. He also remembered how angry Newton was with Paul when they gave the family a demonstration of her skill.

"Soon Hattie will be a better shot than you, Paul, and I suppose you will want to take her with you on your tour this fall?" Newton quipped.

"What do you mean soon? She's already a better shot than I

am, Newton. She never misses, and yes, I do want to take her with me. Would you and Minerva be agreeable to that?"

Minerva answered, "I would be, Paul, but only because you're my brother, and, if you don't mind, I'd like you to take Robert as well, to help keep an eye on her."

That Fall Hattie and Robert left with their Uncle Paul and traveled across the country. At the end of the year, Hattie returned with a substantial amount of prize money, which she generously used to make improvements on the farm.

A bird, landing on the windowsill, fluttered about, startling Lewis and hurling his thoughts back to the present. Turning once again to Hattie, he wondered and prayed, "How long will it be before she awakens? Please, dear Lord, make it soon."

As the days passed with no change in Hattie's condition, everyone began to lose hope, everyone, that was, but Lewis. He refused to leave her side, even at Minerva's insistence. More than once, Minerva would enter Hattie's room and find him kneeling in prayer at her bedside. "What great faith he has, and what a gentle man he is," Minerva thought. Together with Dakota, they marveled at how Lewis spent hours reading to Hattie and talking to her as if she were awake. Once, as they came down the hall, they could hear him singing the last song they had written together and found him sitting on her bed holding her tenderly in his arms. Her head lay gently on his shoulder, and she looked as if she were only asleep. In a voice just above a whisper, Minerva said to Lewis, "Romeo's Juliet could not have looked more beautiful, lyin' in your arms, than Hattie does." Minerva believed whatever kind of love it was that Lewis had for Hattie, it could only be described as timeless.

Dakota asked tenderly, "This seems so hopeless, Lewis, how

long are you goin' to keep up this vigil?"

"As long as it takes, Dakota. I didn't come here to give up, nor did I come here to lose. I'm here because I know the strength of my faith and because I believe in the power of love that exists between us. Hattie will pull through. I know it." Hearing the sincerity and determination in his confidently spoken words was something that Dakota Jayne would never forget.

As Lewis continued to stay at Hattie's side, Laville entered one day wanting to talk. She was not feeling well, and she could not, for the life of her, remember what had happened in the last week. The only memory she had was that Hattie had been hurt badly, but everything else was a blur. She hated when she lost track of time like that, but being afraid everyone would think she was crazy, she shrugged it off as an unfortunate fact of life. "Besides," she thought to herself, "I've got even bigger problems to worry about."

Taking a seat next to Lewis in a chair near Hattie's bedside, they began to reminisce about all that had happened in the past few years. In a gentle voice, he explained the immensity of Hattie's fortune to Laville and the huge responsibility Hattie had. "You must understand, Laville, the Andersons' estate can't even begin to compare to Hattie's fortune. You see, with great wealth like Hattie's, comes great responsibility, and a person must learn that either you rule your wealth or it rules you."

Loving money as she did, Laville wanted to know exactly how much her sister had. "Can you describe how great her fortune is in one word?"

"Immense."

"So, what you're telling me is that neither Hattie nor the rest of us really realize just how much money she has?"

"Exactly. That's exactly right," Lewis replied. Continuing, he said, "Even I wasn't aware of it until just before she married Abner, when James and I finished all the papers and transfers of her holdings. Rebecca and my mother have, without a doubt, two of the largest fortunes in the country, following closely behind the Rockefeller and Carnegie fortunes. The transfer of Rebecca's holdings, which I said are immense, has actually caused quite a stir in financial circles throughout the country. Hattie now owns every kind of business you can think of. Not to mention farms, mills, and factories, all over the country. She is the major stockholder in a shipping line in the East just like I am in the Southern Cross Shipping Line in the South. Knowing what Hattie was given, I can understand why Abner and Jess are so angry. They had the world at their fingertips and lost it all."

"How in the world did Rebecca run such an empire?"

"Rebecca, the refined woman that she is, had absolutely no desire to personally involve herself with the business world. Therefore, she surrounded herself with extremely competent, trustworthy men, who have managed her assets and interests for nearly a quarter of a century. Together, they have increased her fortune several times over, and have made themselves rich in the process."

"Will James be able to handle all of that himself?"

"No, of course not, and he knows that Hattie will still need the help of many trusted men, just as Rebecca has. James will simply oversee everything at the highest level. We spoke this morning, and I've decided to work with him, with Hattie's approval, of course. But, Laville, you haven't forgotten what I told you at Hattie's wedding."

Laville certainly hadn't forgotten what he had told her the day of Hattie's wedding. She could hardly believe it at the time, but now, after several months of going over it in her mind, she was actually looking forward to the challenge. "Of course not, Lewis, and if anyone can do it and make it work, we will."

"I'm really going to need your help."

"Don't worry; whatever it takes, Hattie and I will be with you all the way." She paused for a second then continued. "Mind if I ask you a real personal question?"

"No, of course not."

"How do you handle your mother's empire?"

Exactly as Rebecca has done, and I go right along with her thinking, 'great wealth is only good for the good that it can do'. My intentions have always been to alleviate as much suffering in the world as I can with the fortune the good Lord has blessed me with."

As Laville got up and walked to the window, she felt compelled to tell Lewis about the money problems that were weighing heavily on her mind. Slowly, she began to explain how she had foolishly squandered her fortune, hoping that he, of all people, would understand. "Lewis, you probably won't believe this but I've gone through every dollar I got from the Andersons' estate, and I'm deeply in debt. I've already sold most of their property, and now I'm going to have to sell the farm and the business in town just to break even. I'd have been a lot better off if I had left for New York City as I intended. I guess, Lewis, with the way I've handled money, you must consider me a 'number one fool'."

Laville was right. He was very surprised she was broke, but only because he knew she had been left with considerable wealth. "Mind if I ask what you did with it?"

"Oh, I have things to show for it, including the house in town, which I furnished with only the best things I could buy, and I have bought beautiful clothes and jewels. But along the way, I've made some really bad investments. I'm in such a mess now that I was thinking about asking Hattie to help me."

Seeing the sadness in her face, he walked over and put his arm around her. "Don't do that, Laville. If you need help, let me help you. As soon as Hattie is better and before I begin my plans, let's go to the bank. It'll be tough for a while until I get your assets straightened out, but I'm sure with a little work we can do it and have you back on top within a year, without your having to sell the farm." Taking her hands in his, he turned her to face him. Standing with the golden sunlight streaming in the window and touching her face, he marveled at her beauty. "How could any woman be born so naturally beautiful?" he thought. Then, speaking softly, he said, "I want you to be completely honest with me, Laville."

"All right, Lewis, shoot."

"How much do you owe?" As she told him, he took a deep breath then smiled. "That's nearly a king's ransom," he said jokingly.

"I know it is, Lewis. Are you sure you still want to help?"

Still smiling, he gave her a wink. "Of course, Dear. Actually, forget what I said about going to the bank a moment ago. If you will promise me you'll stay with me and help me through my agonizing dilemma, I'll pay all of it myself."

Laville was astonished and awe stricken. No one had ever been so naturally kind to her in her entire life. She didn't even know what having a friend was like, much less an angel like Lewis. Flustered, she began to protest, "Listen, Lewis, I've got no one to blame but myself. I can't let you do this. It's far too much money. As far as me helping you, you can count on me for that no matter what."

"Then let me do it. Let me help you, and let's make a deal. Help me in the name of love, and I'll do the same for you."

Laville looked away, she still couldn't believe anyone would come to her aid. Her only hope had been to ask Hattie for help, and now, here was Lewis literally saving her life, again.

"Well, will you let me, Laville?" he asked again. "It would mean a lot to me to have the privilege of helping you, and Heaven knows I can certainly afford it."

Laville turned back to face him, "I hope my help will somehow balance or offset what you are proposing to do for me."

Lewis put his arms around her and pulled her to him. "Stand by me through this, and I promise I will never abandon you in any cause you may have now or in the future." She sighed deeply, as he continued, "You know, if you truly want to be a rich woman, let me teach you how to manage money and how to avoid financial pitfalls."

Laville, being bright, caught on quickly to everything he suggested. Never once did Lewis condemn her for her foolishness. Instead, he encouraged her to use her head and to think before she spent anything over one hundred dollars. He cautioned her, "The worse thing a woman can be, Laville, is wealthy, yet foolish with money. You have been blessed with incredible beauty and brains. You already have all the ingredients to make you a successful woman, but you must learn to use your head."

Laville had always known Lewis to be kind, and his genuine concern brought out the best in her. She wanted the best life had to offer and that, of course, took money and plenty of it. The time she spent with Lewis during Hattie's coma was invaluable, and the years that followed would show just how much. For Laville, their friendship would become the most stabilizing influence in her life.

***

Finally, after three long and agonizing weeks for the family, Hattie came out her coma. But had it not been for Lewis's constant love and attention, she might never have survived, much less overcame the loss of her daughter. For the first time in her life, Hattie was totally devastated, not having been able to see Faith or hold her. She was grateful to Laville for having named the child, and said, "I could not have chosen a more perfect name, Laville, and I will never forget your kindness." Laville accepted her gratitude but did not recall the funeral or suggesting the name 'Faith' for Hattie's baby. Then, turning to Lewis with tears in her eyes, Hattie added, "And Lewis, I don't know how I can ever repay you for the love and dedication you've shown to me these past weeks, other than to promise you that I will always come to your aid, no matter what."

Lewis, taking her hand in his, mouthed softly, "I know, Hattie. I'm counting on it."

The next afternoon when Hattie and Lewis were alone, Hattie said matter of factly, "Laville is a regular 'Dr. Jekyll and Mr. Hyde', Lewis. I just don't understand her, and I guess I never will. It is a mystery to me how any one person can be so contrary. One day she'll be her normal agitatin' self, but the next, for some unknown reason, she'll be as sweet as sugar."

Lewis sat on the edge of her bed listening carefully to everything Hattie had to say, when suddenly he remembered how he had once met a doctor in Boston who believed that under certain conditions a person might develop personality problems. The Doctor had said, "All men and women have within them a good side and a bad side. Each person also definitely has a part of them that is feminine and a side that is masculine, regardless of their gender, and sometimes, these things are out of balance." Lewis had found what the Doctor had had said very interesting, but at the same time, he knew that the area in which the Doctor specialized in, psychology, was still in its infancy. No one, including the Doctor himself, knew what would come of this new and groundbreaking field that dealt with the intricate issues of the mind.

During the following week, Hattie regained strength, yet Lewis still wouldn't leave her side. Fortunately, by March 26, 1897, the day Lucinda gave birth to her child, Hattie was well enough to stand at Lucinda's bedside.

Dan Brown, Lucinda's father, waited nervously outside the bedroom door as Laville, Dakota, Minerva, Rebecca and Lucinda's mother, Katherine, sat in chairs across the room, intently watching Doc Cowley as he worked with Lucinda. Together, they held hands and prayed that things would go smoothly. The last thing any of them wanted to see was another tragedy, but unfortunately, as sometimes happens in life, when it rains, it pours.

The delivery was extremely difficult with the child being breach, and Lucinda struggled to give birth. Near the end, she pleaded with Hattie, "Hattie, if anythin' happens to me, please take my baby and raise it as your own."

Hattie wiped the perspiration from Lucinda's forehead. "Now, Lucinda, let's not talk about something like that. You're goin' to be just fine."

Lucinda, wanting to get Hattie's solemn word, squeezed her hand tightly. "Promise me!"

Hattie, seeing the seriousness in her eyes, patted her hand and nodded her head affirmatively. "All right, Lucinda, I promise."

No more than five seconds later, Lucinda cried out in pain and collapsed. Her mother Katherine ran to her side. "Lucinda! Lucinda!" she screamed. "Hold on, Baby!" There was a frail cry and the doctor announced that she had given birth to a tiny redheaded girl.

As Mary cleaned the child, Doc Cowley realized Lucinda was hemorrhaging seriously. He worked frantically but to no avail. The breach birth had seriously injured Lucinda, and try as he may, he just couldn't stop the bleeding, nor could he save her life. In the blink of an eye, she was dead, and everyone in the room sat in silence, devastated.

Rebecca opened the door and tearfully called to Lucinda's father, Dan, who heard his wife crying but couldn't tell what was going on. He had heard the baby cry so he assumed everything was all right, but upon entering the room and seeing that his beautiful Lucinda was gone, he fell to his knees and wept. For next few minutes, everyone in the room including Doc Cowley cried along with the Browns. After all that had happened in the last month, Lucinda's death was almost too much to bear. Mary, with the baby cradled in her arms, stood in awe looking back at the outpour of genuine human emotion. Tears ran down her face as she looked heavenward and cried out, "How much, dear Lord, can this poor family be a takin'?"

The next morning the family stood in the estate's cemetery again, this time surrounding Lucinda's grave. At Hattie's request, Dan and Katherine Brown permitted Lucinda to be buried on the estate, instead of in the Gallatin cemetery, just outside town.

A feeling of gloom hung over the mansion for the next couple weeks, as the family found it hard to get over, not only the death of little Faith but now Lucinda as well.

Katherine and Dan made daily trips to see the baby, and Hattie asked a number of times if they were sure that it was all right for her to raise the child. Katherine, having heard her daughter with her own ears plead with Hattie to raise their grandchild, felt sure they were all doing the right thing. "Besides," she said, "she looks as if she belongs to you, Miss Hattie, both of you havin' red hair and all."

"She gets her red hair from you, Mrs. Brown."

"Nevertheless, Dear, she does favor you, and that will be a blessin' in years to come. What Dan and I have been wonderin', though, is if you've chosen a name for her?"

"I think so, she said softly. How do you feel about Katherine Lucinda?"

Tears filled Katherine's eyes, as her heart was touched. "I like it very much."

Hattie handed the baby to her grandmother. "I found a sheet of paper on Lucinda's desk the day she died. Down one side, she had written several boys' names and circled Daniel; down the other, she had written several girls' names and circled Katherine. She had already chosen the names she wanted; I just wanted to add Lucinda to your name so that the baby will always have a remembrance of her mother, even though I will be the one who raises her."

Katherine was deeply moved by Hattie's thoughtfulness. "I have so little to remember her by, Miss Hattie."

Hattie, giving her a warm smile, knew this was the perfect time to show Katherine the surprise that she had for her. Walking to an easel that was set up in the corner of the parlor where they were talking and removing the cloth, Katherine was shocked to see a remarkable painting of Lucinda that Hattie had recently finished. "This was to be a gift from Lucinda to you on your birthday," Hattie said solemnly.

Looking at her daughter's likeness, Katherine began to cry. "She was so beautiful, and so sweet."

"It's for you, Mrs. Brown. Whenever the pain gets to where you think you can't handle it, you can look at this picture and take solace in the fact that she loved you very much, and despite the pain, know that she is exactly where she needs to be, in the arms of Heavenly Father."

Chapter 8
NO TURNING BACK

BY THE TENDER AGE of sixteen and a half, young Hattie Garland had encountered almost every kind of tragedy imaginable. She had been raped, beaten, and left for dead twice. She had given birth to and suffered the loss of her first child, watched helplessly as her good friend Lucinda died while in childbirth and was now responsible for the baby. All of this on the heels of being given one of the largest fortunes in country, which made her the sole support of her family. Needless to say, God was testing her. But, as all great beings do, she rose to the occasion, persevered where others would have folded, and refused to throw blame. Blame, she would say, "Is what people do to hide their own imperfections." She did all of this while maintaining a positive attitude for the future, even though the past gave her plenty of reason to be bitter. These angelic qualities drew people to her like a magnet, and in the years to come, she would prove herself, over and over again, to be a loyal and devoted wife, mother, grandmother, daughter, sister, and friend.

Having spent endless hours with Hattie growing up, Lewis Alexander Beaumont knew all of this, for that is why he confided in her. He knew she never broke a promise or made a promise lightly, and like Lucinda, his life would be greatly affected by Hattie's strength, love, and devotion. Unlike Lucinda, though, Lewis and Hattie's lives would be forever intertwined.

***

As the family gathered quietly in the parlor, Minerva closed the large double doors behind her and took a seat. It was nearly three weeks after Lucinda's death, and though no one was fully over the shock of her passing, Hattie and Lewis decided it was time to put their plan into motion.

Hattie, trying not to appear nervous, said, "I've called you here tonight for a family conference. Lewis has somethin' personal he needs share with us this evenin'. He has been strugglin' with a problem for years, and after havin' come to a decision on what he wants to do, he needs our love and support to help him get through it." She paused then turned to Mary and George Walsh. "I decided with all we've shared in this house as a family that you two must be included, for I feel we are one family." Again pausing and looking around the room into the faces of her family, she smiled nervously. "Curtis, why don't you take your younger brothers, and go upstairs. I feel this might be a little much for the four of you, but I promise that I will tell you everythin' when you're old enough to understand better." Seeing them leave, she looked back at Lewis, and he gave her a nod, indicating it was time.

Starting slowly, the tone in Hattie's voice became deadly serious. "I want everyone to understand that the secret which is to be shared with you tonight must be kept completely confidential, and if necessary, taken to your grave. If you don't think you're capable of keepin' a confidence like that, please excuse yourself and leave now." She waited a full minute, giving each person a chance to think it over, and as she had hoped, no one left the room.

Members of her family looked at one another puzzled. They wondered what secret could possibly be so important that they would be expected to take to their grave. Finally, Shannon spoke up for the family. "Okay, Hattie, we'll do anythin' you ask, and of course, we'll do anythin' we can to help you, Lewis."

Hattie, hearing them offer their support, was greatly relieved. Turning to Laville, she invited her to take the floor.

Taking Lewis's hand, Laville brought him to the front of the room with her. Then speaking to him, she said, "I believe I speak for all of us when I say you've been like a brother to us ever since we were children. You have our word that we will never divulge anything about what you are going to share with the family tonight. As Hattie and I told you earlier, Lewis, we will all stand behind you."

Lewis gratefully thanked Laville then walked over and shook Shannon's hand. "Thank you, Shannon for your support. I hope that when I've finished telling you what I intend to do you will still stand by me."

Shannon, somewhat perplexed, asked, "As long as we've been friends, Lewis, if you had a problem why didn't you come to me?"

"I just couldn't, Shannon. Not until I spoke to Hattie and Laville first." Lewis anxiously looked around the study, knowing they were about to hear something they weren't going to like, let alone understand. "When I finish telling you my problem and solution, I promise I'll answer any questions you have as straightforwardly and as honestly as possible." Pausing, he glanced at the clock on the fireplace mantel and took a deep breath.

Curious and impatient, John asked pointedly, "What is it, Lewis? Have you killed somebody or somethin'?"

"No, John, it's nothing like that. And I'm not in any trouble with the law either."

"If it's so dad blamed important, why haven't you gone to your Ma?" inquired Robert.

"I have several times but she does not think there is much chance."

Minerva, tired of the constant questions, scolded her sons. "You boys quit questionin' Lewis and hush up. For God's sake, give him a chance to tell you."

Taking one last glance at Hattie for strength, Lewis breathed deeply and said softly but plainly, "It all started several years ago. I was in a meeting with some clients in New York and had not been feeling very well at all. After several meetings I met with one of my cousins who is a doctor. After doing several test he could not figure out why I was beginning to feel so weak for no apparent reason." Pausing a moment, Lewis looked into the eyes of the family members. "I'm afraid I have been to see several doctors the last few months and they tell me that I do not have much longer to live."

Silence so thick you could have cut through it with a knife covered the room like a blanket. Faces seemed frozen in time. What Lewis had said came across completely honest and deadly serious.

After what seemed like an eternity, James was the first to speak, and he spoke as slowly, quietly, and as distinctly as Lewis had. "Lewis, I'm afraid this comes as a great shock. I've known you for years and have never heard anything about this. That is absolutely terrible."

Shaking his head, John was dumbfounded. Gathering his

thoughts, he raised his hand slightly to get Lewis's attention. "Have you told you're Mother about this?"

Standing there a moment looking at the family, Lewis finally nodded his head. "A few months ago I went to the doctor with my mother and he gave us the bad news. But that is not the entire story so let me finish telling you everything."

Shannon, having been best friends with Lewis since they were children stood to his feet and walked to him. Hugging him for a long moment Shannon stepped back, "We will be here for you and anything that you need."

"Thank you Shannon."

Taking his seat again he and the family waited for Lewis to continue.

"As I said there is more to the story. One thing that I don't think any of you know, I have a cousin. Her name is Lou she is the daughter of General Alexander from back east. She will be coming out here with Hattie's permission and will be helping Hattie as she is very business savvy having been to some of the best schools on the east coast and will be inheriting my fortune after I pass away. She will also be helping my mother with things after I pass on."

Rebecca, standing up, cleared her throat and interjected, "Perhaps this is a little too delicate for mixed company."

"Please, Rebecca, don't leave!" Lewis pleaded. "I need your input probably more than anyone. Coming from one of the wealthiest families here in the South I can think of no one better than you to help her and Hattie."

Hearing the sincerity in his voice, Rebecca sat back down and said emphatically, "All right, Lewis, I know how important this is to you. I will do everything I can to help her" Replying in a calm voice,

Lewis was grateful to have Rebecca's support. "I can't thank you enough, Rebecca. Hattie, Laville, and I have gone over this for months."

"Just when will your cousin be arriving?" Shannon asked curiously.

"She will be arriving tomorrow actually."

Laville, sensing Lewis needed someone to take the pressure off him, addressed the family. "Lewis, came to Hattie and I and asked us to take Lou under our wing for the next six months or so with Mother, Cody, and Rebecca's help so that we can not only help her find her place among our family but help her stand on her own two feet especially with everything that is happening."

Dakota, sitting in the back next to James, raised her hand cautiously. Lewis, seeing her, quickly invited her to speak. "What has brought you to this decision Lewis to leave your entire fortune to your cousin?"

"Well to start off my Aunt and Uncle passed away not too long ago and I know that things have been hard and lonely for Lou. I also know that mother is going to need a lot of help after I pass getting used to things and I think Lou is the perfect answer to both problems. I know that she has a tender heart and yet is strong enough to be one person you would not want to trifle with."

"So what is expected of us, Hattie," James asked supportively. "I still have doubts as to how this will work, but it appears as though the three of you have planned every detail, long before you included us. So, tell us, just where do we fit in?"

"Lewis needs a place to stay," Hattie replied, "a place that will be private and safe. Since he has already been stayin' with us over the past couple of months while I recovered from losing Faith and then Lucinda, I have asked him to stay here."

Lewis, hoping dearly that the answer would be yes, looked at the family and asked cautiously, "Hattie and Laville have suggested that I stay here at the Estate among you, but I will only do that if all of you are willing to accept and support me."

"This is Hattie's home now," Rebecca replied, "and she can share it with whomever she pleases. As for your living here, it is certainly all right with me. Whatever you decide, I promise you I will support you to the best of my ability."

"Thank you, Rebecca, that's all I ask."

Lewis smiled. "I'll step on the veranda and leave you to consider all that I have proposed to you this evening and whether or not you will be able to accept my cousin and everything that this will be entailing." Leaving the room and closing the door behind him, he walked out onto the veranda and made his way to its edge. He was perspiring and his heart was racing, so the cool April air felt good on his face. Looking heavenward, he saw the full moon, which was lighting the veranda as if it were early morning. "I can't turn back now," he said to himself, "no matter what the cost."

Inside the house, everyone was quiet, lost deep in thought. Hattie went to her mother and placing her hand on her shoulder said, "Mama, none of us are perfect, and nearly everyone has somethin' they don't want known." Turning to the rest of the family, she raised her voice so that everyone could hear. "I know what Lewis has asked of us is a lot, but where else can he turn?"

With Hattie's words echoing through her mind, Minerva suddenly felt a calmness that she recognized as the spirit of the Lord descending upon her. As it touched her heartstrings and impressed on her mind that which was right, Minerva truly began to understand

Lewis's predicament, as she too had secrets she didn't want known. Speaking with new found conviction, she told her children, "Hattie's right. Lewis needs us. I've always taught you that when it comes to important decisions, you must think it through and pray for guidance before making a decision." Pausing, she looked around at every member of her family. "Well, after receivin' inspiration on this issue, I feel that we need to help him."

Laville, thankful for her mother's support, added, "Hattie and I have spent a lot of time thinking and praying about this as well, and we've decided that we aren't going to let Lewis fight this battle alone. Now, what about the rest of you?"

Shannon spoke first, and everyone listened intently. "Lewis is like a member of our family no matter what he chooses to do. No matter the outcome of his actions, it doesn't change that basic fact. I think I speak for everyone when I say that we agree with the three of you; we can't let him face this alone."

"Thank you Shannon," Hattie replied gratefully. She was very relieved that Lewis had the family's support. Taking a deep breath, she continued, "The last part of Lewis's plan is that he must change all of his holdings and his fortune to Louise Alexander, she will be empowered with all that Lewis has."

The family agreed they would make every effort to make Lewis's transition as easy as possible, and everyone went to the veranda. Finding Lewis staring out into the clear night sky, James addressed him for the family. "I'm sure this isn't going to be easy for you, Lewis, and may seem almost impossible at times, but I promise you, we will do our very best to support you, no matter what."

"That's all I ask, James. And when you see my cousin Lou I

hope that you can bring her into your hearts just as you have me all of my life. I hope you won't think any less of me as my health quickly begins to fail."

As the family returned to the parlor, Shannon stayed behind with Lewis and Hattie. Shannon, still deeply concerned, wanted to say one last thing to his longtime friend. "We've been through a lot, Lewis, and we've been closer than brothers. My hope for you is that you find the peace you've been searchin' for and that you'll be happy with your decision."

Lewis, grateful for the friendship between them, smiled, and as they had done thousands of times, they gave each other a brotherly embrace.

Tired, Shannon said goodnight, leaving Hattie and Lewis standing on the edge of the veranda. The night seemed unusually calm, and in the stillness, crickets and tree frogs could be heard singing. "Well," Hattie said with relieved look on her face, "the worst is over. You have a new beginning."

Holding her hand, he sighed deeply. "There's 'no turning back' now."

"True," she said solemnly, "tomorrow really will be 'the first day of the rest of your life.'"

Chapter 9
EARTH ANGEL

THE NEXT MORNING Pansy waited at the train station as the people began to disembark the train and made their way across the platform to their various destinations. Pansy waited eagerly, scanning the crowd for Louise Alexander.

Pansy's sister had become involved with a man who was in the military and had a very promising career. Years later they had their only child Louise. With some wise investments that her father had made and the passing of both of her parents, Louise, had been left very well off. She had used her fortune to help those in need.

Finally as the crowd began to clear, Pansy spotted Louise standing in a flowing green dress that accented her long golden blond hair.

After a quick embrace, Pansy took a step back to look Louise over from head to toe. "My, my, my. I'm quite surprised that some young man has not tried to snatch you up yet."

Blushing slightly, Lou smiled, "Well it isn't like they haven't tried, Aunt Pansy. I just have not found the right man yet I guess. Besides, since the passing of Mama and Daddy, I just haven't had time for men."

"Well, I know you will just love it here. I just wish it could be under better circumstances," Pansy said as a slight desperation crept into her voice.

"What exactly is going on? The telegram that I got from Lewis didn't say very much," Lou inquired.

"Well, honey, sometimes things are best said in person rather than by correspondence," Pansy replied in a hushed voice.

Lou stared at Pansy. She didn't know exactly what was going on but she knew it was not good . The trip to the mansion was beautiful. Entering Silver Creek Estate, Lou sighed at the natural beauty.

Finally, as they approached the steps leading up the front porch, Lou saw Hattie, Laville and Minerva waiting to greet her. From that exact moment she had a feeling that her life would never again be the same. Lou strongly believed that there are some moments in people's lives when a certain chapter ends and another begins.. Walking up the steps, she took Hattie's hand and gently embraced her.

Hattie returned the embrace and felt too that this was one of those life changing moments. Standing back, she looked at Lou and thought to herself. "Well, well, if looks like Laville may have a run for her money when it comes to looks. Lou is absolutely gorgeous."

Stepping forward and hugging Lou, Minerva was the first to speak, "Well Louise, how was your trip?"

"Please call me Lou, Mrs. Morran."

"Well I will, as long as you call me ether Minerva or Mother Morran."

"Yes, Mother Morran." Lou responded as she turned her attention back to Hattie.

"And you, I understand, are Miss Hattie. I knew that from the letters I received from Lewis, who spoke so highly of you. I can see why he regards you as an Earth Angel."

Hattie smiled. She had always been so close to Lewis and had known that the love between them was only that of sole mates could have. The kind of love the poets have spoken about through the ages. That's why she dreaded being separated from Lewis for six long months.

"I have to tell you your cousin means very much to me. I just am truly sorry that things have come to this." Hattie said, lost in her thoughts.

At that moment Lewis appeared at the doorway. Making their way inside, they came into the parlor. It was time for Lou to learn why she had come.

"So why don't we drop the small talk Lewis and tell me why you sent me such an urgent telegram." Lou said.

"Well, it's hard to get much more obvious than that," Lewis said as he walked over and took a seat next to Lou.

Hattie knew that this was a very serious moment. She closed the doors to the parlor. Lewis spent two hours telling Lou everything.

Over the next six months, Lewis's health had become steadily worse and Doc Cowley could do nothing more for him. Lewis had chosen Lou as his soul heir. She at his death would receive his entire fortune. This when combined with Lou's own fortune would make her fortune considerably large. Finally on October 20, 1879, Doc Cowley came out of Lewis's bedroom.

As he reached Hattie, she took him by the hands; "Don't beat around the bush Doc, tell me the truth. How much time does he have left?"

Looking into her green eyes, Doc Cowley replied, "I'm not positive—minutes maybe hours—but he will not last the night. He has requested that you come in first, Hattie, followed by the rest of the family. All you can do now is say goodbye."

Standing there a moment Hattie's was heartbroken. She knew that this day had been coming for six months but nothing had really prepared her. Nodding her head she went into the room while the doctor told the others.

Lewis was sitting up in bed. He had a heavenly glow surrounding him even though his skin was pale. Patting a spot on the bed next to him, he encouraged Hattie to take a seat.

"It appears Hattie, that the time has come for us to say our final goodbyes. I have a few things I want to tell you before the rest of the family comes in, so please give me a moment to tell you everything that is in my heart."

Hattie slowly nodded her head.

"I want you to know how special you are. I believe that it is not the end, only the next step. Know that I will always be with you. My thoughts are with you always. I have truly treasured every moment of time that I've had with you. And, I know you're your fortune has been both a blessing and a curse."

"Just as sure as in times of old your future is surely *Written in the Stars*. You need to make sure Hattie, that you always choose what is right over what is easy. I think that you should find a business partner. Never try and do anything all by yourself. Take strength in your family and their encouragement."

A tear softly ran down Hattie's cheek. She had known Lewis all of her life and she was so saddened that she was now losing him. First Faith, now Lewis, Hattie wondered when on earth it was going to end.

That's the way life is and Hattie needed to learn to accept that.

Just as she was about to speak she heard the rest of the family enter, led by Shannon. He took a seat on the other side of Lewis and was so filled with sadness that there were tears in his eyes. Lewis looking into Shannon's eyes knew his feelings, and patted his hand gently.

"Shannon, we have been friends all of our lives. Now, I leave it to you to take care of Hattie and the family."

"I," Shannon stammered. "I will."

Lewis, staring at him for another long moment, turned his attention to Lou who was standing at the end of the bed. "Remember Lou, what we have talked about. I'm relying on you the most. Take care of things for me after I'm gone."

Lou nodded her head slowly. At that moment, there was an indescribable feeling of peace. One they had never felt before.

Lying down, Lewis began to feel his life slipping away. Turing slightly, he looked to a light that began to illuminate behind Hattie. As the family watched, his life essence drifted away into eternity.

Moments later, Lewis found himself dressed in a white suit standing next to a beautiful woman. She had long blond hair and bright blue eyes. She too was dressed in white and offered him words of comfort, "Don't worry Lewis, I will be with them from time to time, as will some of the others that have been pre destined to help them."

"Who are you?" Lewis asked curiously.

"My name is Angelique, and I am one of the angels that God has assigned to your family. I'm here to help you say goodbye to your earthly existence and take you home. First we have to help you say goodbye to the ones you love."

Instantly they were at Lewis's funeral at the family cemetery. They watched as James gave a prayer where he thanked God for allowing Lewis into their lives. Reverend Walker spoke conducted the service. As the service came to an end the family members came up and shared their personal feelings about Lewis.

As the funeral concluded, Angelique turned to Lewis. "It's time Lewis for us to return home."

"Am I going to Heaven or Hell?"

Smiling, Angelique shook her head gently. This same question had been asked of her many times. "Don't worry, you are going somewhere were you will feel completely comfortable."

***

Shadowed in darkness, hidden in the brush, a lone figure peered over the ridge watching as the family laid Lewis to rest. An evil smile crossed the dark figures lips as the near silent words fell softly in the breeze.

"Now to only get rid of Lou, then that fortune will fall into my hands."

The figure turned and disappeared into the brush.

About the Author

Alex Skyler Alexander is a bright, motivated thirty four year old male who has been working on a novel which was the combined effort between him and his late father Shayne Alexander. Forced to Love is the first in a series of novels about the very colorful life of Sky's great-grandmother, Hattie.

For more information about Sky Alexander make sure to check out his website and signup for his free News Letter with special deal only to only the select members.

Please Sign up for Sky Alexander's newsletter:
http://www.romancefictionbooks.com/?page_id=82

Also check out Sky Alexander Facebook Page:
https://www.facebook.com/skyalexander79

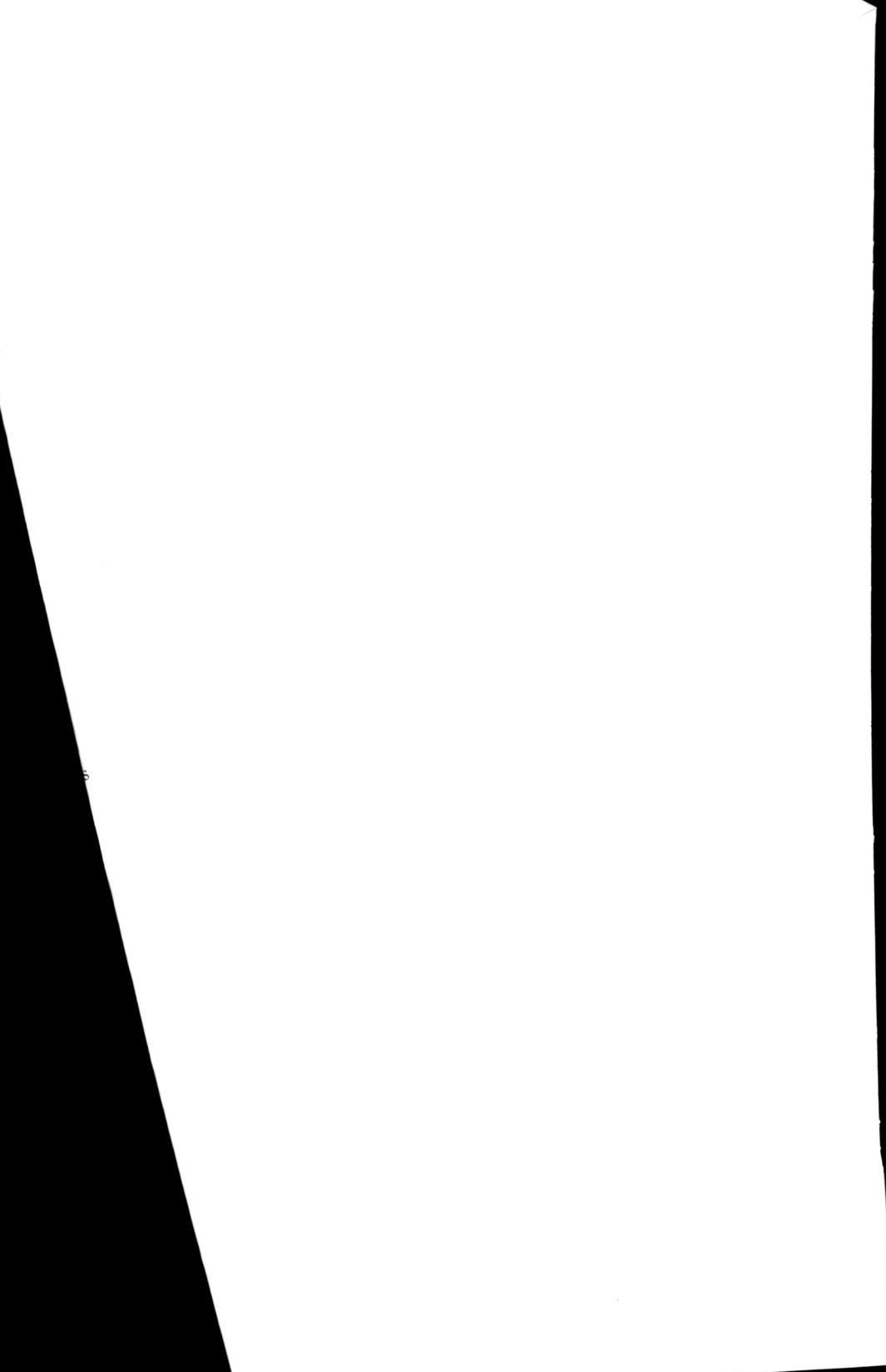

About the Author

Alex Skyler Alexander is a bright, motivated thirty four year old male who has been working on a novel which was the combined effort between him and his late father Shayne Alexander. Forced to Love is the first in a series of novels about the very colorful life of Sky's great-grandmother, Hattie.

For more information about Sky Alexander make sure to check out his website and signup for his free News Letter with special deals only to only the select members.

Please Sign up for Sky Alexander's newsletter:
http://www.romancefictionbooks.com/?page_id=82

Also check out Sky Alexander Facebook Page:
https://www.facebook.com/skyalexander79

Other Books in the Fires of Love & Hate series:

Forced to Love (Book 1)
(Digital) March 1, 2014
(Printed) April 1, 2014

Falling in Love (Book 2)
(Digital) May 1, 2014
(Printed) June 1, 2014

Hate to Love (Book 3)
(Digital) July 1, 2014
(Printed) August 1, 2014

Death of Love (Book 4)
(Digital) September 1, 2014
(Printed) October 1, 2014

Romancing the Heart (Book 5)
(Digital) November 1, 2014
(Printed) December 1, 2014

World Wind Romance (Book 6)
(Digital) January 1, 2015
(Printed) February 1, 2015

Forgiving Romance (Book 7)
(Digital) March 1, 2015
(Printed) April 1, 2015

Broken Promises (Book 8)
(Digital) May 1, 2015
(Printed) June 1, 2015

Shattered Dreams (Book 9)
(Digital) July 1, 2015
(Printed) August 1, 2015

The Price of Intrigue (Book 10)
(Digital) September 1, 2015
(Printed) October 1, 2015

On Course with Destiny (Book 11)
(Digital) November 1, 2015
(Printed) December 1, 2015

Confessions of the Heart (Book 12)
(Digital) January 1, 2016
(Printed) February 1, 2016